Copyright - 2020 -

All rights reserved.

The content contained within this book may not be reproduced, duplicated or transmitted without direct written permission from the author or the publisher.

Under no circumstances will any blame or legal responsibility be held against the publisher, or author, for any damages, reparation, or monetary loss due to the information contained within this book. Either directly or indirectly.

Legal Notice:

This book is copyright protected. This book is only for personal use. You cannot amend, distribute, sell, use, quote or paraphrase any part, or the content within this book, without the consent of the author or publisher.

Disclaimer Notice:

Please note the information contained within this document is for educational and entertainment purposes only. All effort has been executed to present accurate, up to date, and reliable, complete information. No warranties of any kind are declared or implied. Readers acknowledge that the author is not engaging in the rendering of legal, financial, medical or professional advice. The content within this book has been derived from various sources. Please consult a licensed professional before attempting any techniques outlined in this book.

By reading this document, the reader agrees that under no circumstances is the author responsible for any losses, direct or indirect, which are incurred as a result of the use of information contained within this document, including, but not limited to, - errors, omissions, or inaccuracies.

TABLE OF CONTENTS

INTRODUCTION	11
1. BENEFITS OF SMART AIR FRYER OVEN	15
2. FUNCTIONS OF SMART OVEN AIR FRYER	17
3. BREAKFAST RECIPES	19
1. BREAKFAST CHICKEN STRIPS	20
2. CITRUS BLUEBERRY MUFFINS	21
3. PB &J DONUTS	22
4. BREAKFAST BAKED APPLE	23
5. SUNNY SIDE UP EGG TARTS	24
6. HEALTHY SPINACH SCRAMBLE	25
7. HEALTHY VEGAN SCRAMBLE	26
8. EGGS IN ZUCCHINI NESTS	27
9. PROTEIN EGG CUPS	28
10. PUMPKIN PANCAKES	29
11. SHRIMP FRITTATA	30
12. TUNA SANDWICHES	31
13. CLOUD EGGS	32
14. CHICKEN & ZUCCHINI OMELET	33
15. ZUCCHINI FRITTERS	34
16. ONION OMELET	35
17. EGG CUPS WITH BACON	36
18. ALMOND CRUST CHICKEN	37
19. ZUCCHINI MUFFINS	38
20. JALAPENO BREAKFAST MUFFINS	39
21. SIMPLE EGG SOUFFLÉ	40
22. VEGETABLE EGG SOUFFLÉ	41
23. ASPARAGUS FRITTATA	42
24. SPICY CAULIFLOWER RICE	43
25. BROCCOLI STUFFED PEPPERS	44
26. ZUCCHINI NOODLES	45
27. MUSHROOM FRITTATA	46
28. EGG MUFFINS	47
29. BLUEBERRY BREAKFAST COBBLER	48

TABLE OF CONTENTS

30.	YUMMY BREAKFAST ITALIAN FRITTATA	49
31.	SAVORY CHEESE AND BACON MUFFINS	50
32.	BEST AIR-FRIED ENGLISH BREAKFAST	51
33.	SAUSAGE AND EGG BREAKFAST BURRITO	52
34.	FRENCH TOAST STICKS	53
35.	HOME-FRIED POTATOES	54
36.	HOMEMADE CHERRY BREAKFAST TARTS	55
37.	SAUSAGE AND CREAM CHEESE BISCUITS	56
38.	FRIED CHICKEN AND WAFFLES	57
4.	**POULTRY RECIPES**	**59**
39.	PERFECT CHICKEN BREASTS	60
40.	RANCH GARLIC CHICKEN WINGS	61
41.	RANCH CHICKEN THIGHS	62
42.	TACO RANCH CHICKEN WINGS	63
43.	SIMPLE CAJUN CHICKEN WINGS	64
44.	SIMPLE AIR FRIED CHICKEN	65
45.	BUFFALO WINGS	66
46.	HONEY LIME CHICKEN WINGS	67
47.	SIMPLE CHICKEN DRUMSTICKS	68
48.	HEALTHY CHICKEN WINGS	69
49.	THAI CHICKEN THIGHS	70
50.	CHICKEN PATTIES	71
51.	CAJUN SEASONED CHICKEN DRUMSTICKS	72
52.	HONEY GARLIC CHICKEN	73
53.	SRIRACHA CHICKEN WINGS	74
54.	SWEET & SPICY CHICKEN WINGS	75
55.	GINGER GARLIC CHICKEN	76
56.	SALT AND PEPPER WINGS	77
57.	PARMESAN CHICKEN WINGS	78
58.	WESTERN CHICKEN WINGS	79
59.	PERFECT CHICKEN THIGHS DINNER	80
60.	PERFECTLY SPICED CHICKEN TENDERS	81
61.	CHICKEN MEATBALLS	82

TABLE OF CONTENTS

62. HOMEMADE BREADED NUGGET IN DORITOS	83
63. CHICKEN BREAST	84
64. BREADED CHICKEN WITHOUT FLOUR	85
65. BARBECUE WITH CHORIZO AND CHICKEN	86
66. ROASTED THIGH	87
67. COXINHA FIT	88
68. ROLLED TURKEY BREAST	89
69. CHICKEN IN BEER	90
70. CHICKEN FILLET	91
71. CHICKEN WITH LEMON AND BAHIAN SEASONING	92
72. BASIC BBQ CHICKEN	93
73. BASIC NO FRILLS TURKEY BREAST	94
74. FAIRE-WORTHY TURKEY LEGS	95
75. HERB AIR FRIED CHICKEN THIGHS	96
76. QUICK & EASY LEMON PEPPER CHICKEN	97
77. SPICY JALAPENO HASSEL BACK CHICKEN	98
78. TASTY HASSEL BACK CHICKEN	99
79. WESTERN TURKEY BREAST	100
80. LEMON PEPPER TURKEY BREAST	101
81. TENDER TURKEY LEGS	102
5. MEAT RECIPES	**103**
82. BULLET-PROOF BEEF ROAST	104
83. PORK AND POTATOES	105
84. PORK AND FRUIT KEBABS	106
85. STEAK AND VEGETABLE KEBABS	107
86. SPICY GRILLED STEAK	108
87. GREEK VEGETABLE SKILLET	109
88. LIGHT HERBED MEATBALLS	110
89. BROWN RICE AND BEEF-STUFFED BELL PEPPERS	111
90. BEEF AND BROCCOLI	112
91. BEEF AND FRUIT STIR-FRY	113
92. GARLIC PUTTER PORK CHOPS	114
93. CAJUN PORK STEAKS	115

TABLE OF CONTENTS

94. CAJUN SWEET-SOUR GRILLED PORK	116
95. PORK LOIN WITH POTATOES	117
96. ROASTED CHAR SIEW (PORK BUTT)	118
97. ASIAN PORK CHOPS	119
98. MARINATED PORK CHOPS	120
99. STEAK WITH CHEESE BUTTER	121
100. MADEIRA BEEF	122
101. CREAMY PORK AND ZUCCHINIS	123
102. JUICY STEAK BITES	124
103. GREEK LAMB CHOPS	125
104. EASY BEEF ROAST	126
105. BEEF JERKY	127
106. SIMPLE BEEF PATTIES	128
107. PORK TAQUITOS	129
108. PANKO-BREADED PORK CHOPS	130
109. CRISPY ROAST GARLIC-SALT PORK	131
110. BEEF ROLLS	132
111. HOMEMADE CORNED BEEF WITH ONIONS	133
112. DUO CRISP RIBS	134
113. ROAST BEEF	135
114. BASIC PORK CHOPS	136
115. BREADED PORK CHOPS	137
116. BEEF AND BALSAMIC MARINADE	138
117. CRISPY BRATS	139
118. BASIL PORK CHOPS	140
119. BEEF AND RADISHES	141
120. HERBED PORK CHOPS	142
121. BEEF TENDERLOIN	143
122. HONEY MUSTARD PORK TENDERLOIN	144
6. FISH AND SEAFOOD	**145**
123. BUTTER TROUT	146
124. PESTO ALMOND SALMON	147
125. GARLIC LEMON SHRIMP	148

TABLE OF CONTENTS

126. AIR-FRIED CRAB STICKS	149
127. AIR FRY CAJUN SALMON	150
128. E-Z CATFISH	151
129. FISH NUGGETS	152
130. GRILLED SHRIMP	153
131. HONEY & SRIRACHA TOSSED CALAMARI	154
132. SALMON CROQUETTES	155
133. SPICY COD	156
134. AIR FRIED LOBSTER TAILS	157
135. AIR FRYER SALMON	158
136. SIMPLE SCALLOPS	159
137. 3-INGREDIENT AIR FRYER CATFISH	160
138. PECAN-CRUSTED CATFISH	161
139. FLYING FISH	162
140. AIR FRYER FISH TACOS	163
141. BACON WRAPPED SCALLOPS	164
142. QUICK FRIED CATFISH	165
143. AIR-FRIED HERBED SHRIMP	166
144. BREADED FLOUNDER	167
145. SIMPLE HADDOCK	168
146. BREADED HAKE	169
147. SESAME SEEDS COATED TUNA	170
148. CHEESE AND HAM PATTIES	171
149. AIR-FRIED SEAFOOD	172
150. FISH WITH CHIPS	173
151. CRUMBLY FISHCAKES	174
152. BACON WRAPPED SHRIMP	175
153. CRAB LEGS	176
154. FISH STICKS	177
155. CRUSTY PESTO SALMON	178
156. SALMON PATTIES	179
157. CAJUN SALMON	180
158. BUTTERY COD	181

TABLE OF CONTENTS

159. SESAME TUNA STEAK	182
160. LEMON GARLIC SHRIMP	183
161. FOIL PACKET SALMON	184
162. FOIL PACKET LOBSTER TAIL	185
163. AVOCADO SHRIMP	186
164. CITRUSY BRANZINI ON THE GRILL	187
165. CAJUN-SEASONED LEMON SALMON	188
166. GRILLED SALMON FILLETS	189
167. CHEESY BREADED SALMON	190
168. COCONUT CRUSTED SHRIMP	191
169. RICE FLOUR COATED SHRIMP	192
170. BUTTERED SCALLOPS	193
7. SNACK AND APPETIZER	**195**
171. BUTTERNUT SQUASH WITH THYME	196
172. CHICKEN BREASTS IN GOLDEN CRUMB	197
173. YOGURT CHICKEN TACOS	198
174. FLAWLESS KALE CHIPS	199
175. CHEESE FISH BALLS	200
176. VERMICELLI NOODLES & VEGETABLES ROLLS	201
177. BEEF BALLS WITH MIXED HERBS	202
178. ROASTED PUMPKIN SEEDS	203
179. BUTTERY PARMESAN BROCCOLI FLORETS	204
180. SPICY CHICKPEAS	205
181. ROASTED PEANUTS	206
182. ROASTED CASHEWS	207
183. FRENCH FRIES	208
184. ZUCCHINI FRIES	209
185. SPICY CARROT FRIES	210
186. CINNAMON CARROT FRIES	211
187. SQUASH FRIES	212
188. AVOCADO VEGETABLE FRIES	213
189. DILL PICKLE FRIES	214
190. MOZZARELLA STICKS	215

TABLE OF CONTENTS

191. TORTILLA CHIPS	216
192. FLAX SEED CHIPS	217
193. SALTED HAZELNUTS	218
194. BAGUETTE BREAD	219
195. YOGURT BREAD	220
196. SUNFLOWER SEED BREAD	221
197. DATE BREAD	222
198. DATE & WALNUT BREAD	223
199. BROWN SUGAR BANANA BREAD	224
200. CINNAMON BANANA BREAD	225
201. BANANA & WALNUT BREAD	226
202. BANANA & RAISIN BREAD	227
203. 3-INGREDIENTS BANANA BREAD	228
204. YOGURT BANANA BREAD	229
205. SOUR CREAM BANANA BREAD	230
206. PEANUT BUTTER BANANA BREAD	231
207. CHOCOLATE BANANA BREAD	232
208. ALLSPICE CHICKEN WINGS	233
209. FRIDAY NIGHT PINEAPPLE STICKY RIBS	234
210. EGG ROLL WRAPPED WITH CABBAGE AND PRAWNS	235
211. SESAME GARLIC CHICKEN WINGS	236
212. SAVORY CHICKEN NUGGETS WITH PARMESAN CHEESE	237
8. VEGETABLES	**239**
213. FLAVORED ASPARAGUS	240
214. AVOCADO FRIES	241
215. SPAGHETTI SQUASH TOTS	242
216. CINNAMON BUTTERNUT SQUASH FRIES	243
217. CHEESY ROASTED SWEET POTATOES	244
218. SALTY LEMON ARTICHOKES	245
219. ASPARAGUS & PARMESAN	246
220. CORN ON COBS	247
221. ONION GREEN BEANS	248
222. DILL MASHED POTATO	249

TABLE OF CONTENTS

- 223. CREAM POTATO — 250
- 224. CHARD WITH CHEDDAR — 251
- 225. CHILI SQUASH WEDGES — 252
- 226. HONEY CARROTS WITH GREENS — 253
- 227. SOUTH ASIAN CAULIFLOWER FRITTERS — 254
- 228. SUPREME AIR-FRIED TOFU — 255
- 229. CRISPY POTATOES AND PARSLEY — 256
- 230. GARLIC TOMATOES — 257
- 231. EASY GREEN BEANS AND POTATOES — 258
- 232. GREEN BEANS AND TOMATOES — 259

9. DESSERTS — 261

- 233. DONUTS PUDDING — 262
- 234. LEMON BARS — 263
- 235. COCONUT DONUTS — 264
- 236. BLUEBERRY CREAM — 265
- 237. BLACKBERRY CHIA JAM — 266
- 238. MIXED BERRIES CREAM — 267
- 239. BLOOD ORANGE AND GINGER CHEESECAKE — 268
- 240. SPICED PEAR SAUCE — 269
- 241. HONEY FRUIT COMPOTE — 270
- 242. APRICOT CRUMBLE WITH BLACKBERRIES — 271
- 243. APPLE & CINNAMON PIE — 272
- 244. MINI CHEESECAKES — 273
- 245. VANILLA CHEESECAKE — 274
- 246. RICOTTA CHEESECAKE — 275
- 247. PECAN PIE — 276
- 248. FRUITY CRUMBLE — 277
- 249. CHERRY CLAFOUTIS — 278
- 250. APPLE BREAD PUDDING — 279
- 251. MASALA CASHEW — 280

CONCLUSION — 281

INTRODUCTION

The Breville Smart Air Fryer Oven is one of the most advanced air fryer ovens on the planet, thanks to its digital controls and the ability to adjust the heating elements for optimal results. But perhaps the best feature of the Breville Smart Air Fryer is its ability to cook by convection. Unlike normal cooking, convection produces the most uniform heat possible, circulating the heated air.

The Breville Smart Oven Air Fryer is the latest member of an array of different models of highly efficient, innovative and user-friendly cooking devices that condense the functions and capabilities of several kitchen appliances into one. Manufactured and primarily marketed by the Breville Property Limited, USA, this magnificent device boasts of high-class technology, providing impressive versatility and many other unique features that have ultimately made them consumer favorites.

It employs the power of super convection to ensure adequate and efficient cooking and reduces cooking time by thirty percent. The Element iQ technology uses six separate core heating elements to enhance uniformity of cooking. It also remembers your last settings on the oven.

FEATURES OF THE BREVILLE SMART OVEN AIR FRYER

Apart from its use of advanced technology and versatility, one of the most attractive features of the Breville Smart Oven Air Fryer is its sheer size. With its interior measuring one cubic foot, this behemoth can bear large quantities of food [up to fourteen pounds], which is quite impressive for a single oven. This, coupled with alluring and durable hardware and sophisticated built-in executive software functions, makes it worth the buy.

The hardware includes a pizza pan, a wire rack, a broiling rack, an enamel roasting pan, an air fry/dehydrate basket and a crumb tray. Other physical features include a power cord, ventilation slots, door sensor, oven light and a front control section which houses an LCD screen and a control panel.

On this control panel, you will find a couple of dials and buttons such as the Temperature Control dial, the Time dial, the Function button, the Oven Light button, the Convection button, the Phase Cook button, the Frozen Foods button and the Temperature Conversion button. Some of these buttons perform more than one function. For example, the Function button is used as both the Select/Confirm dial and the Rotate/Remind dial. The Temperature Control dial also serves the Volume Adjustment function.

Accessories such as bamboo cutting board, pizza stone and pizza crisper pan, are sold separately and they add to the luxury of the Breville Smart Oven Air Fryer.

The Led Crystal Display screen provides effortless manipulation and navigation of the various built-in functions. This screen, together with the oven light and the control panel, makes it easy to use the Breville Smart Oven Air Fryer at any time of the day. From toast to roast to dehydrate, it offers visuals into the various cooking options as well all other functions and settings.

HOW TO USE: BASIC TIPS AND PRECAUTIONS

After purchasing your Breville Smart Oven Air, remove all packing materials and cards and carefully discard. Clean the trays, racks and pans with soft sponge immersed in warm water. Leave to dry adequately before use. The interior should also be cleaned but with just moist soft sponge. When the interior is well dried, insert the crumb tray.

Remove the power cord from the pack and plug into a grounded outlet. On plugging in, you will hear the oven alert sound and the LCD screen backlight will be turned on and display the different function options with the indicator on Toast function. Then, with Select/Confirm dial, select the Pizza function. Next, press the Start/stop button. This will make the button backlight glow red, the LCD screen glow orange and the oven alert sound to be heard.

This orange screen will also display a blinking PREHEATING notification. This means the device is in the preheating cycle. On completion of the preheating cycle, the alert sounds once more. This done, the oven will automatically start a new cooking cycle and display the timer which begins a countdown. Once this cooking cycle is over, the oven alert will sound again, the Start/Stop button backlight turns off and the LCD screen backlight becomes white. You can now begin to use the oven.

This process may take up to twenty minutes. It is essential that this be done before doing any cooking so as to remove the protective materials present on the heating elements.

After this initial preparatory setup, you can now begin use your oven.

First, insert the wire rack into the appropriate position in the interior of the oven. The rack positions for each cooking setting are printed on the left-hand side of the oven door window. Next, select the desired cooking setting on the LCD screen by turning the Select/Confirm dial. For all cooking settings, the preset cooking temperature is displayed. You can manually adjust this cooking temperature by using the Temperature dial. To increase temperature, turn to the right; turn to the left to reduce the temperature. For the Toast and Bagel settings, the Darkness Level is also indicated above the temperature indicator. The preset cooking time is displayed at the bottom right of the LCD screen. Turn the Time dial right or left to increase or decrease cooking time respectively. For the Toast and Bagel settings, the number of slices is displayed. The cooking temperature and time can be adjusted even during cooking.

Settings such as Bagel, Broil, Dehydrate, Proof, Reheat, Toast and Warm do not require a preheat cycle. For these settings, simply place the food on the wire rack or tray. Ensure the food is placed as near the center of the oven as possible for uniform cooking. Close the oven door and press the Start/Stop button. The Start/Stop button backlight glows red and the LCD screen glows orange, the timer begins countdown. The oven alert sounds and the screen glows white on completion of the cooking cycle.

For other settings that require preheat, press the Start/Stop button, the LCD screen will then display a blinking PREHEATING notification. When the preheating cycle is over, the oven alert sounds, the PREHEATING notification stops and the timer starts. Place the food in the oven and wait till food is done.

1. BENEFITS OF SMART AIR FRYER OVEN

The smart fryer oven comes with several benefits, some of which are as follows:

HEALTHY AND FATTY FOODS

The smart fryer oven works with transfer technology. Blow hot air into the cooking pan to cook food quickly and evenly on all sides. When frying your food in a smart fryer, you need a tablespoon or less than a tablespoon of oil. One bowl of fries requires only one tablespoon of oil and makes the fries crisp on the outside and tender on the inside. If you are among the people who like fried food but are worried about extra calories, this kitchen appliance is for you.

OFFERS 13-IN-1 OPERATION

The Breville smart air fryer oven offers 13 functions in one device. These functions are Toast, Bagel, Toast, Bake, Broil, Hot, Pizza, Proof, Air Fry, Reheat, Cookie, Slow Cook, and Dehydrate. These are all smart programs that offer flexible cooking.

SAFE TO USE

The smart fryer oven cooking appliances is one of the safest compared to a traditional one. While cooking your food, the appliance is closed on all sides; because of this, there is no risk of hot oil splashing on your finger. This is one of the safest frying methods compared to another traditional frying method. A narrow cooking method gives you a splatter-free cooking experience. Smart IQ technology makes the device safer, and there is no possibility of burning food. Smart IQ automatically detects and adjusts the temperature of the item according to the needs of the recipe.

EASY TO CLEAN

The Breville smart fryer oven is made of reinforced stainless steel, and the inner body is coated with non-stick materials. All interior accessories are dishwasher safe. You can wash it in a dishwasher or also wash it with soapy water. The smart fryer cooks your food in much less oil. Less oil means less chaos.

CARE AND CLEANING

1. Before starting the cleaning process, ensure that the power cord has been unplugged. Allow your oven and accessories to cool to room temperature before beginning the cleaning process.

2. Clean the oven body with a soft, damp cleaning sponge during the cleaning process. When cleaning the glass door, you can use a glass cleaner and a plastic cleaning pad to clean. Do not use metal coatings that can scratch the surface of your oven.

3. The inner body of the oven consists of a non-stick coating. Use a soft, damp sponge to clean the inside of the oven. Apply detergent to a sponge and do not apply it directly to the body of the oven. You can also use a mild spray solution to avoid staining.

4. Before cleaning the components, make sure the oven has cooled down to room temperature and then wipe gently with a soft damp cloth or sponge.

5. Dust the crumb tray with a soft, damp sponge. You can use a non-abrasive liquid cleaner. Apply detergent to a sponge and clean the disc.

6. To clean a frying pan, immerse it in warm soapy water and wash it with the help of a plastic frying pan or a soft sponge.

7. Remember to always dry all accessories thoroughly before placing them in the oven. Put the crumb tray in place before plugging the oven into its socket. Now your oven is ready for the next use.

Adding SIRT-rich foods to the food day is not at all a bad idea. It can bring health benefits, but this is just another restrictive diet like so many others, with nothing special worth the buzz created around it.

The Sirtfood Diet is suitable for people with perseverance and discipline nutrition-loving people with background knowledge.

The Sirtfood Diet is not suitable for people who have a hard time consuming only a few calories every day.

Many advisers reveal which other foods are suitable for the sirt food diet and which other foods are combined with them. These can be helpful in planning daily food preparation better and thus make it easier. Because a comprehensive knowledge of sirtuins, their effects, and how to best integrate them into your daily diet increases your stamina.

Relaxation is also an essential part of the sirt food diet. In stressful situations, the hormone cortisol is released, which, together with insulin, stimulates blood sugar levels and causes the body to feel hungry during periods of rest. Mainly due to the calorie reduction, one should avoid stressful situations in everyday life as much as possible. Small activities to balance out like a little walk in the fresh air can work wonders.

2. FUNCTIONS OF SMART OVEN AIR FRYER

Breville smart air fryer comes with 13 smart cooking functions. These functions are as follows:

1. TOAST: This function is used to toast the bread. Makes your bread brown and crisp on the outside. It is also used for English muffins and frozen waffles.

2. BAGEL: This function is used to crisp the inside of the cut bun and also to make light toast on the outside. It is also ideal for baking thick slices of bread or potatoes.

3. ROAST: With this function, you can cook poultry, minced meat, fish, vegetables, and sausages. Also great for browning the tops of grits, pots, and desserts.

4. BAKE: This function is used for baking your favorite cakes, muffins, and brownies.

5. ROAST: With this function, you can cook your favorite meat and poultry. You can also cook a whole chicken. Baking makes food tender and juicy inside.

6. HEAT: This function helps prevent the growth of bacteria. Keeps your oven temperature 160 ° C / 70 ° C.

7. PIZZA: This feature melts the cheese topping and browns on the top during pizza slices.

8. TEST: With this function, you can create the ideal environment to test the dough, slices of bread, and pizza.

9. AIRFRY: With these functions, you can make your food crisp and golden. This function is ideal for French fries.

10. HEAT: This function is ideal for reheating frozen food or food scraps without browning or drying the food.

11. COOKIES: This function is used for baking your favorite cookies and other baked goods.

12. BUY COOKING: This function is used for cooking your food for a long time at low temperatures.

13. DEHYDRATATION: This function is used to dry food without heating or to cook it. It is

ideal for dehydrating your favorite fruits.

CARE AND CLEANING

1. Before starting the cleaning process, ensure that the power cord has been unplugged. Allow your oven and accessories to cool to room temperature before beginning the cleaning process.

2. Clean the oven body with a soft, damp cleaning sponge during the cleaning process. When cleaning the glass door, you can use a glass cleaner and a plastic cleaning pad to clean. Do not use metal coatings that can scratch the surface of your oven.

3. The inner body of the oven consists of a non-stick coating. Use a soft, damp sponge to clean the inside of the oven. Apply detergent to a sponge and do not apply it directly to the body of the oven. You can also use a mild spray solution to avoid staining.

4. Before cleaning the components, make sure the oven has cooled down to room temperature and then wipe gently with a soft damp cloth or sponge.

5. Dust the scrap tray with a sponge. You can use a non-abrasive liquid cleaner. Apply detergent to a sponge and clean the disc.

6. To clean a frying pan, immerse it in warm soapy water and wash it with the help of a plastic frying pan or a soft sponge.

7. Remember to always dry all accessories thoroughly before placing them in the oven. Put the crumb tray in place before plugging the oven into its socket. Now your oven is ready for the next

3. BREAKFAST RECIPES

1. BREAKFAST CHICKEN STRIPS

 **PREPARATION TIME**
5 MINUTES

 **COOK TIME**
12

 **SERVING**
4

INGREDIENTS

- 1 teaspoon paprika
- 1 tablespoon cream
- 1 lb. chicken fillet
- ½ teaspoon salt
- ½ teaspoon black pepper

DIRECTIONS

1. Cut the chicken fillet into strips.
2. Sprinkle the chicken fillets with salt and pepper.
3. Preheat the air fryer to 365 degree Fahrenheit.
4. Place the butter in the air basket tray and add the chicken strips. Cook the chicken strips for 6-minutes.
5. Turn the chicken strips to the other side and cook them for an additional 5-minutes.
6. After strips are cooked, sprinkle them with cream and paprika, then transfer them to serving plates. Serve warm.

Nutrition: Calories: 245, Total Fat: 11.5g, Carbs: 0.6g, Protein: 33g

2. CITRUS BLUEBERRY MUFFINS

PREPARATION TIME
15 MINUTES

COOK TIME
15

SERVING
3-4

INGREDIENTS

- 2 ½ cups cake flour — 312g / 11oz
- ½ cup sugar — 113.5 / 4oz
- ¼ cup light cooking oil such as avocado oil
- ½ cup heavy cream — 4.15oz
- 1 cup fresh blueberries — 227g / 8oz
- 2 eggs
- Zest and juice from 1 orange
- 1 tsp. pure vanilla extract
- 1 tsp. brown sugar for topping

Handwritten notes:
- 100g butter
- 140g sugar
- 2 large eggs
- 140g yogurt
- 1 tsp vanilla
- 2 tbspn milk
- 250g plain flour
- 2 tsp baking powder
- 1 tsp bicarbonate soda
- 125g blueberries

DIRECTIONS

1. Start by combining the oil, heavy cream, eggs, orange juice and vanilla extract in a large bowl then set aside.
2. Separately combine the flour and sugar until evenly its mixed then pour little by little into the wet ingredients.
3. Combine until well blended but be careful not to over-mix.
4. Preheat your breville smart air fryer toast oven at 320°F
5. Fold the blueberries into the batter and split into cupcake holders, preferably, silicone cupcake holders as you won't have to grease them. Alternatively, you can use cupcake paper liners on any cupcake holders/ tray you could be having.
6. Dust the tops with the brown sugar and pop the muffins in the fryer.
7. Bake for about 12 minutes. Use a toothpick to check for readiness. When the muffins have evenly browned and an inserted toothpick comes out clean, they are ready.
8. Take out the muffins and let cool.
9. Enjoy!

Handwritten notes: 7 muffins, 320F for 12 minutes, rotate 1 Sum

Nutrition: Calories: 289 kcal/Cal, Carbs: 12.8 g, Fat: 32 g, Protein: 21.1 g

3. PB &J DONUTS

PREPARATION TIME 15 MINUTES	**COOK TIME** 12	**SERVING** 4

INGREDIENTS

For the Donuts:
- 1 ¼ cups all-purpose flour
- ½ tsp. baking soda
- ½ tsp. baking powder
- 1/3 cup sugar
- ½ cup buttermilk
- 1 large egg
- 1 tsp. pure vanilla extract
- 3 tbsp. unsalted, melted and divided into 2+1
- ¾ tsp. salt

For the Glaze:
- 2 tbsp. milk
- ½ cup powdered sugar
- 2 tbsp. smooth peanut butter
- Sea salt to taste
- For the Filling:
- ½ cup strawberry or blueberry jelly

DIRECTIONS

1. Mix all the dry ingredients for the donut in a large bowl.
2. Separately combine the egg, buttermilk, melted butter and vanilla extract.
3. Make a small well at the middle of the dry ingredients and pour in the egg mixture. Use a fork to join the ingredients then finish off with a spatula.
4. Place the dough on a floured surface and knead the dough. It will start out sticky but as you knead, it's going to come together.
5. Roll out the dough to make a ¾ inch thick circle. Use a cookie cutter, or the top part of a cup to cut the dough into rounds.
6. Place the donuts on a parchment paper and then into your Breville smart air fryer toast oven.
7. Cook for 12 minutes at 350°F.
8. Use a pastry bag to fill the donuts with jelly.
9. Combine the glaze ingredients and drizzle on top of the donuts.
10. Enjoy!

Nutrition: Calories: 430 kcal/Cal Carbs: 66.8 g Fat: 14.6 g Protein: 9.1 g

4. BREAKFAST BAKED APPLE

PREPARATION TIME
10 MINUTES

COOK TIME
20

SERVING
2

INGREDIENTS

- 1 apple
- 2 tbsp. raisins
- 2 tbsp. walnuts, chopped
- ¼ tsp. nutmeg
- ¼ tsp. ground cinnamon
- 1 ½ tsp. margarine
- ¼ cup water

DIRECTIONS

1. Start by setting your Breville smart air fryer toast oven to 350°F.
2. Cut the apple in half and gently spoon out some of the flesh.
3. Place the apple halves on your Breville smart air fryer toast ovens frying pan.
4. Mix the raisins, walnuts, nutmeg, cinnamon and margarine in a bowl and divide equally between the apple halves.
5. Pour the water into the pan and cook for 20 minutes.
6. Enjoy!

Nutrition: Calories: 161 kcal/Cal Carbs: 23.7 g Fat: 7.8 g Protein: 2.5g

5. SUNNY SIDE UP EGG TARTS

PREPARATION TIME	COOK TIME	SERVING
15 MINUTES	20	2

INGREDIENTS

- 4 eggs
- ¾ cup shredded Gruyere cheese (or preferred cheese)
- 1 sheet of puff pastry
- Minced chives for topping

DIRECTIONS

1. Start by flouring a clean surface then gently roll out your sheet of puff pastry and divide it into four equal squares.
2. If you have a small Breville smart air fryer toast oven, start with two squares but if it's big enough, go ahead and place the squares on the basket and cook for about 8-10 minutes or until they turn golden brown.
3. Whilst still in the basket, gently make an indentation at the center of each square and sprinkle 2-4 tablespoons of shredded cheese in the well then crack an egg on top.
4. Cook for 5-10 minutes or to desired doneness.
5. Remove from Breville smart air fryer toast oven, sprinkle with chives and you are ready to eat!

Nutrition: Calories: 403 kcal/Cal Carbs: 10.8 g Fat: 29.4 g Protein: 24.6 g

6. HEALTHY SPINACH SCRAMBLE

PREPARATION TIME
8 MINUTES

COOK TIME
30

SERVING
2

INGREDIENTS

- 3 egg whites
- 1 cup (packed) spinach
- 1 onion, chopped
- 2 tbsp. extra virgin olive oil
- ½ tsp. onion powder
- ½ tsp. garlic powder
- 1 tsp. turmeric powder
- Ground pepper to taste

DIRECTIONS

1. Preheat your Breville smart air fryer toast oven to 350°F.
2. Beat the egg whites and oil in a large bowl. Add in the fresh ingredients and mix until well combined then set the bowl aside.
3. Lightly grease your Breville smart air fryer toast oven's frying pan and transfer the egg mixture into the pan.
4. Cook in the fryer for about 10 minutes or until done to desire.
5. Serve hot.

Nutrition: Calories: 285 kcal/Cal Carbs: 12.3 g Fat: 21.6 g Protein: 13 g

7. HEALTHY VEGAN SCRAMBLE

PREPARATION TIME
8 MINUTES

COOK TIME
30

SERVING
3

INGREDIENTS

- 2 large potatoes, cut into cubes
- 1 tofu block, cut into cubes
- 1 broccoli, divided into florets
- 1 large onion, chopped
- 2 tbsp. dark soy sauce
- 2 tbsp. extra virgin olive oil, divided into 1+1
- ½ tsp. onion powder
- ½ tsp. garlic powder
- 1 tsp. turmeric powder
- Ground pepper to taste

DIRECTIONS

1. Start by marinating the tofu in 1 tablespoon of olive oil onion, garlic, turmeric and onion powders then set aside.
2. Drizzle the potatoes with the remaining tablespoon of olive oil and toss with pepper and cook in the Breville smart air fryer toast oven for 15 minutes at 400°F. Halfway through cook time, toss the potatoes to allow even cooking.
3. Toss the potatoes once more then mix in the marinated tofu, reserving the leftover liquid and cook for another 15 minutes at 370°F.
4. Toss the broccoli florets in the leftover marinade. If it's too little, drizzle with some soy sauce and toss to ensure all the florets are evenly covered.
5. When the potato-tofu mixture has 5 minutes of cooking time left, add in the broccoli.
6. Serve hot.

Nutrition: Calories: 319 kcal/Cal Carbs: 50.4 g Fat: 10.9 g, Protein: 8 g

8. EGGS IN ZUCCHINI NESTS

 **PREPARATION TIME**
5 MINUTES

 **COOK TIME**
7

 **SERVING**
4

INGREDIENTS

- 4 teaspoons butter
- ½ teaspoon paprika
- ½ teaspoon black pepper
- ¼ teaspoon sea salt
- 4-ounces cheddar cheese, shredded
- 4 eggs
- 8-ounces zucchini, grated

DIRECTIONS

1. Grate the zucchini and place the butter in ramekins.
2. Add the grated zucchini in ramekins in the shape of nests. Sprinkle the zucchini nests with salt, pepper, and paprika.
3. Beat the eggs and pour over zucchini nests.
4. Top egg mixture with shredded cheddar cheese.
5. Preheat the air fryer basket and cook the dish for 7-minutes.
6. When the zucchini nests are cooked, chill them for 3-minutes and serve them in the ramekins.

Nutrition: Calories: 221, Total Fat: 17.7g, Carbs: 2.9g, Protein: 13.4g

9. PROTEIN EGG CUPS

PREPARATION TIME
10 MINUTES

COOK TIME
9

SERVING
2

INGREDIENTS

- 3 eggs, lightly beaten
- 4 tomato slices
- 4 tsp cheddar cheese, shredded
- 2 bacon slices, cooked and crumbled
- Pepper
- Salt

DIRECTIONS

1. Spray silicone muffin molds with cooking spray.
2. Whisk the egg with pepper and salt in a bowl. Preheat the air fryer to 350 F.
3. Pour eggs into the silicone muffin molds. Divide cheese and bacon into molds.
4. Top each with tomato slice and place in the air fryer basket.
5. Cook for 9 minutes.
6. Serve and enjoy.

Nutrition: Calories 67 Fat 4 g Carbohydrates 1 g Sugar 0.7 g Protein 5.1 g Cholesterol 125 mg

10. PUMPKIN PANCAKES

PREPARATION TIME
15 MINUTES

COOK TIME
12

SERVING
2

INGREDIENTS

- 1 square puff pastry
- 3 tablespoons pumpkin filling
- 1 small egg, beaten

DIRECTIONS

1. Roll out a square of puff pastry and layer it with pumpkin pie filling, leaving about ¼-inch space around the edges.
2. Cut it up into 8 equal sized square pieces and coat the edges with beaten egg.
3. Press "Power Button" of Air Fry Oven and turn the dial to select the "Air Fry" mode.
4. Press the Time button and again turn the dial to set the Cooking Time: to 12 minutes.
5. Push the Temp button and rotate the dial to set the temperature at 355 degrees F.
6. Press "Start/Pause" button to start.
7. When the unit beeps to show that it is preheated, open the lid.
8. Arrange the squares into a greased "Sheet Pan" and insert in the oven.
9. Serve warm.

Nutrition: Calories 109 Total Fat 6.7 g Saturated Fat 1.8 g Cholesterol 34 mg Sodium 87 mg Total Carbs 9.8 g Fiber 0.5 g Sugar 2.6 g Protein 2.4 g

11. SHRIMP FRITTATA

 **PREPARATION TIME**
10 MINUTES

 **COOK TIME**
15

 **SERVING**
2

INGREDIENTS

- 4 eggs
- ½ teaspoon basil, dried
- Cooking spray
- Salt and black pepper to the taste
- ½ cup rice, cooked
- ½ cup shrimp, cooked, peeled, deveined and chopped
- ½ cup baby spinach, chopped
- ½ cup Monterey jack cheese, grated

DIRECTIONS

1. Mix eggs with salt, pepper and basil and whisk.
2. Grease your air fryer's pan with cooking spray and add rice, shrimp and spinach.
3. Add eggs mix, sprinkle cheese all over and cook in your air fryer at 350 degrees F for 10 minutes.
4. Divide among plates and serve for breakfast.
5. Enjoy!

Nutrition: Calories 162, Fat 6, Fiber 5, Carbs 8, Protein 4

12. TUNA SANDWICHES

PREPARATION TIME
10 MINUTES

COOK TIME
5

SERVING
2

INGREDIENTS

- 16 ounces canned tuna, drained
- ¼ cup mayonnaise
- 2 tablespoons mustard
- 1 tablespoons lemon juice
- 2 green onions, chopped
- 3 English muffins, halved
- 3 tablespoons butter
- provolone cheese

DIRECTIONS

1. In a bowl, mix tuna with mayo, lemon juice, mustard and green onions and stir. Grease muffin halves with the butter,
2. Place them in preheated air fryer and bake them at 350 degrees F for 4 minutes. Spread tuna mix on muffin halves,
3. top each with provolone cheese, return sandwiches to air fryer and cook them for 4 minutes,
4. Divide among plates and serve for breakfast right away.
5. Enjoy!

Nutrition: Calories: 182, Fat: 4, Fiber: 7, Carbs: 8, Protein: 6

13. CLOUD EGGS

PREPARATION TIME
8 MINUTES

COOK TIME
4

SERVING
2

INGREDIENTS

- 1 teaspoon butter
- 2 eggs

DIRECTIONS

1. Separate the eggs and the egg yolks from the egg whites.
2. Then whisk the egg whites with the aid of the hand mixer until the white peaks are strong.
3. After that, spread the butter over the air fryer basket tray.
4. Heat up the air fryer to 300 F.
5. Get the egg white peaks medium clouds in the ready air fryer basket tray.
6. In the Air Fryer, position the basket tray and cook the cloud eggs for two minutes.
7. Take away the basket from the air Fryer after this, place the egg yolks in the middle of each egg cloud, and return the basket to the air fryer.
8. Cook the dish for an extra 2 minutes.
9. Then extract the cooked meal from the basket and serve.

Nutrition: Calories 80, Fat 6.3, Fiber 0, Carbs 0.3, Protein 5.6

14. CHICKEN & ZUCCHINI OMELET

PREPARATION TIME	COOK TIME	SERVING
15 MINUTES	35	2

INGREDIENTS

- eggs
- ½ cup milk
- Salt and ground black pepper, as required
- 1 cup cooked chicken, chopped
- 1 cup Cheddar cheese, shredded
- ½ cup fresh chives, chopped
- ¾ cup zucchini, chopped

DIRECTIONS

1. Add the eggs, milk, salt and black pepper and beat well.
2. Add the remaining ingredients and stir to combine.
3. Place the mixture into a greased baking pan. Press "Power Button" of Air Fry Oven and turn the dial to select the "Air Bake" mode.
4. Press the Time button and again turn the dial to set the Cooking Time: to 35 minutes.
5. Now push the Temp button and rotate the dial to set the temperature at 315 degrees F. Press "Start/Pause" button to start.
6. When the unit beeps to show that it is preheated, open the lid.
7. Arrange pan over the "Wire Rack" and insert in the oven.
8. Cut into equal-sized wedges and serve hot.

Nutrition: Calories: 209 Total Fat: 13.3 g Saturated Fat: 6.3 g, Cholesterol: 258 mg, Sodium: 252 mg Total Carbs: 2.3 g Fiber: 0.3 g Sugar: 1.8 g Protein: 9.8 g

15. ZUCCHINI FRITTERS

PREPARATION TIME 15 MINUTES	**COOK TIME** 7	**SERVING** 2

INGREDIENTS

- 10½ oz. zucchini, grated and squeezed
- oz. Halloumi cheese
- ¼ cup all-purpose flour
- 2 eggs
- 1 teaspoon fresh dill, minced
- Salt and ground black pepper, as required

DIRECTIONS

1. In a large bowl and mix together all the ingredients. Make a small-sized fritter from the mixture.
2. Press "Power Button" of Air Fry Oven and turn the dial to select the "Air Fry" mode. Press the Time button and again turn the dial to set the Cooking Time: to 7 minutes.
3. Now push the Temp button and rotate the dial to set the temperature at 355 degrees F. Press "Start/Pause" button to start.
4. When the unit beeps to show that it is preheated, open the lid. Arrange fritters into grease "Sheet Pan" and insert in the oven.
5. Serve warm.

Nutrition: Calories: 253 Total Fat: 17.2 g Saturated Fat: 11 g Cholesterol: 121 mg Sodium: 333 mg Total Carbs: 10 g Fiber: 1.1 g Sugar: 2.7 g Protein: 15.2 g

16. ONION OMELET

PREPARATION TIME
10 MINUTES

COOK TIME
15

SERVING
2

INGREDIENTS

- eggs
- ¼ teaspoon low-sodium soy sauce
- Ground black pepper, as required
- 1 teaspoon butter
- 1 medium yellow onion, sliced
- ¼ cup Cheddar cheese, grated

DIRECTIONS

1. In a skillet, melt the butter over medium heat and cook the onion and cook for about 8-10 minutes.
2. Remove from the heat and set aside to cool slightly.
3. Meanwhile, in a bowl, add the eggs, soy sauce and black pepper and beat well.
4. Add the cooked onion and gently, stir to combine. Place the zucchini mixture into a small baking pan.
5. Press "Power Button" of Air Fry Oven and turn the dial to select the "Air Fry" mode.
6. Press the Time button and again turn the dial to set the cooking time to 5 minutes.
7. Now push the Temp button and rotate the dial to set the temperature at 255 degrees F. Press "Start/Pause" button to start.
8. When the unit beeps to show that it is preheated,
9. Open the lid. Arrange pan over the "Wire Rack" and insert in the oven.
10. Cut the omelet into 2 portions and serve hot.

Nutrition: Calories: 222 Total Fat: 15.4 g Saturated Fat: 6.9 g Cholesterol: 347 mg Sodium: 264 mg Total Carbs: 6.1 g Fiber: 1.2 g Sugar: 3.1 g Protein: 15.3 g

17. EGG CUPS WITH BACON

PREPARATION TIME
10 MINUTES

COOK TIME
15

SERVING
4

INGREDIENTS

- ½ teaspoon paprika
- 1 tablespoon butter
- ¼ teaspoon salt
- ½ teaspoon dried dill
- eggs
- oz. bacon

DIRECTIONS

1. In the blender pot, beat the eggs. Paprika, salt, and dried dill are then added. Using the hand blender, carefully mix the egg mixture.
2. Then pour the butter over four ramekins.
3. Cut the bacon and put it in cup shape in ready-made ramekins.
4. Dress the egg mix with bacon in the middle of each ramekin.
5. Put Air fryer at 360 F.
6. Put the ramekins in the Air fryer and cover it.
7. Cook for 15 minutes.
8. When the time is finished, the mixture of eggs and bacon should be delicious.
9. Take out the egg cups and serve.

Nutrition: Calories 319, Fat 25.1, Fiber 0.1, Carbs 1.2, Protein 21.4

18. ALMOND CRUST CHICKEN

PREPARATION TIME
10 MINUTES

COOK TIME
25

SERVING
2

INGREDIENTS

- 2 chicken breasts, skinless and boneless
- 1 tbsp. Dijon mustard
- 2 tbsp. mayonnaise
- ¼ cup almonds
- Pepper
- Salt

DIRECTIONS

1. Add almond into the food processor and process until finely ground. Transfer almonds on a plate and set aside.
2. Mix together mustard and mayonnaise and spread over chicken.
3. Coat chicken with almond and place into the air fryer basket and cook at 350 F for 25 minutes
4. . Serve and enjoy.

Nutrition: Calories 409 Fat 22 g Carbohydrates 6 g Sugar 1.5 g Protein 45 g Cholesterol 134 mg

19. ZUCCHINI MUFFINS

PREPARATION TIME
10 MINUTES

COOK TIME
20

SERVING
8

INGREDIENTS

- 6 eggs
- 4 drops stevia
- 1/4 cup Swerve
- 1/3 cup coconut oil, melted
- 1 cup zucchini, grated
- 3/4 cup coconut flour
- 1/4 tsp ground nutmeg
- 1 tsp ground cinnamon
- 1/2 tsp baking soda

DIRECTIONS

1. Preheat the air fryer to 325 F.
2. Add all ingredients except zucchini in a bowl and mix well.
3. Add zucchini and stir well.
4. Pour batter into the silicone muffin molds and place into the air fryer basket.
5. Cook muffins for 20 minutes
6. Serve and enjoy.

Nutrition: Calories 136, Fat 12 g, Carbs 1 g, Protein 4 g

20. JALAPENO BREAKFAST MUFFINS

PREPARATION TIME
10 MINUTES

COOK TIME
15

SERVING
8

INGREDIENTS

- 5 eggs
- 1/3 cup coconut oil, melted
- 2 tsp baking powder
- 3 tbsp erythritol
- 3 tbsp jalapenos, sliced
- 1/4 cup unsweetened coconut milk
- 2/3 cup coconut flour
- 3/4 tsp sea salt

DIRECTIONS

1. Preheat the air fryer to 325 F.
2. In a large bowl, mix together coconut flour, baking powder, erythritol, and sea salt.
3. Stir in eggs, jalapenos, coconut milk, and coconut oil until well combined.
4. Pour batter into the silicone muffin molds and place into the air fryer basket.
5. Cook muffins for 15 minutes
6. Serve and enjoy.

Nutrition: Calories 125, Fat 12 g, Carbs 7 g, Protein 3 g

21. SIMPLE EGG SOUFFLÉ

PREPARATION TIME
5 MINUTES

COOK TIME
8

SERVING
2

INGREDIENTS

- 2 eggs
- 1/4 tsp chili pepper
- 2 tbsp heavy cream
- 1/4 tsp pepper
- 1 tbsp parsley, chopped
- Salt

DIRECTIONS

1. In a bowl, whisk eggs with remaining gradients.
2. Spray two ramekins with cooking spray.
3. Pour egg mixture into the prepared ramekins and place into the air fryer basket.
4. Cook soufflé at 390 F for 8 minutes
5. Serve and enjoy.

Nutrition: Calories 116, Fat 10 g, Carbs 1.1 g, Protein 6 g

22. VEGETABLE EGG SOUFFLÉ

PREPARATION TIME
10 MINUTES

COOK TIME
20

SERVING
4

INGREDIENTS

- 4 large eggs
- 1 tsp onion powder
- 1 tsp garlic powder
- 1 tsp red pepper, crushed
- 1/2 cup broccoli florets, chopped
- 1/2 cup mushrooms, chopped

DIRECTIONS

1. Sprinkle four ramekins with cooking spray and set aside.
2. In a bowl, whisk eggs with onion powder, garlic powder, and red pepper.
3. Add mushrooms and broccoli and stir well.
4. Pour egg mixture into the prepared ramekins and place ramekins into the air fryer basket.
5. Cook at 350 F for 15 minutes Make sure soufflé is cooked if soufflé is not cooked then cook for 5 minutes more.
6. Serve and enjoy.

Nutrition: Calories 91, Fat 5.1 g, Carbs 4.7 g, Protein 7.4 g

23. ASPARAGUS FRITTATA

PREPARATION TIME
10 MINUTES

COOK TIME
10

SERVING
4

INGREDIENTS

- 6 eggs
- 3 mushrooms, sliced
- 10 asparagus, chopped
- 1/4 cup half and half
- 2 tsp butter, melted
- 1 cup mozzarella cheese, shredded
- 1 tsp pepper
- 1 tsp salt

DIRECTIONS

1. Toss mushrooms and asparagus with melted butter and add into the air fryer basket. Cook mushrooms and asparagus at 350 F for 5 minutes Shake basket twice.
2. Meanwhile, in a bowl, whisk together eggs, half and half, pepper, and salt. Transfer cook mushrooms and asparagus into the air fryer baking dish. Pour egg mixture over mushrooms and asparagus.
3. Place dish in the air fryer and cook at 350 F for 5 minutes or until eggs are set. Slice and serve.

Nutrition: Calories 211, Fat 13 g, Carbs 4 g, Protein 16 g

24. SPICY CAULIFLOWER RICE

PREPARATION TIME
10 MINUTES

COOK TIME
22

SERVING
2

INGREDIENTS

- 1 cauliflower head, cut into florets
- 1/2 tsp cumin
- 1/2 tsp chili powder
- 6 onion spring, chopped
- 2 jalapenos, chopped
- 4 tbsp olive oil
- 1 zucchini, trimmed and cut into cubes
- 1/2 tsp paprika
- 1/2 tsp garlic powder
- 1/2 tsp cayenne pepper
- 1/2 tsp pepper
- 1/2 tsp salt

DIRECTIONS

1. Preheat the air fryer to 370 F.
2. Add cauliflower florets into the food processor and process until it looks like rice.
3. Transfer cauliflower rice into the air fryer baking pan and Drizzle with half oil.
4. Place pan in the air fryer and cook for 12 minutes, stir halfway through.
5. Heat the remaining oil in a small pan over medium heat.
6. Add zucchini and cook for 5-8 minutes
7. Add onion and jalapenos and cook for 5 minutes
8. Add spices and stir well. Set aside.
9. Add cauliflower rice in the zucchini mixture and stir well.
10. Serve and enjoy.

Nutrition: Calories 254, Fat 28 g, Carbs 12.3 g, Protein 4.3 g

25. BROCCOLI STUFFED PEPPERS

PREPARATION TIME
10 MINUTES

COOK TIME
40

SERVING
2

INGREDIENTS

- 4 eggs
- 1/2 cup cheddar cheese, grated
- 2 bell peppers cut in half and remove seeds
- 1/2 tsp garlic powder
- 1 tsp dried thyme
- 1/4 cup feta cheese, crumbled
- 1/2 cup broccoli, cooked
- 1/4 tsp pepper
- 1/2 tsp salt

DIRECTIONS

1. Preheat the air fryer to 325 F.
2. Stuff feta and broccoli into the bell peppers halved.
3. Beat egg in a bowl with seasoning and pour egg mixture into the pepper halved over feta and broccoli.
4. Place bell pepper halved into the air fryer basket and cook for 35-40 minutes
5. Top with grated cheddar cheese and cook until cheese melted.
6. Serve and enjoy.

Nutrition: Calories 340, Fat 22 g, Carbs 12 g, Protein 22 g

26. ZUCCHINI NOODLES

PREPARATION TIME
10 MINUTES

COOK TIME
44

SERVING
3

INGREDIENTS

- 1 egg
- 1/2 cup parmesan cheese, grated
- 1/2 cup feta cheese, crumbled
- 1 tbsp thyme
- 1 garlic clove, chopped
- 1 onion, chopped
- 2 medium zucchinis, trimmed and spiralized
- 2 tbsp olive oil
- 1 cup mozzarella cheese, grated
- 1/2 tsp pepper
- 1/2 tsp salt

DIRECTIONS

1. Preheat the air fryer to 350 F.
2. Add spiralized zucchini and salt in a colander and set aside for 10 minutes. Wash zucchini noodles and pat dry with a paper towel.
3. Heat the oil in a pan over medium heat. Add garlic and onion and sauté for 3-4 minutes
4. Add zucchini noodles and cook for 4-5 minutes or until softened.
5. Add zucchini mixture into the air fryer baking pan. Add egg, thyme, cheeses. Mix well and season.
6. Place pan in the air fryer and cook for 30-35 minutes
7. Serve and enjoy.

Nutrition: Calories 435, Fat 29 g, Carbs 10.4 g, Protein 25 g

27. MUSHROOM FRITTATA

PREPARATION TIME
10 MINUTES

COOK TIME
13

SERVING
1

INGREDIENTS

- 1 cup egg whites
- 1 cup spinach, chopped
- 2 mushrooms, sliced
- 2 tbsp parmesan cheese, grated
- Salt

DIRECTIONS

1. Sprinkle pan with cooking spray and heat over medium heat. Add mushrooms and sauté for 2-3 minutes Add spinach and cook for 1-2 minutes or until wilted.
2. Transfer mushroom spinach mixture into the air fryer pan. Beat egg whites in a mixing bowl until frothy. Season it with a pinch of salt.
3. Pour egg white mixture into the spinach and mushroom mixture and sprinkle with parmesan cheese. Place pan in air fryer basket and cook frittata at 350 F for 8 minutes
4. Slice and serve.

Nutrition: Calories 176, Fat 3 g, Carbs 4 g, Protein 31 g

28. EGG MUFFINS

PREPARATION TIME
10 MINUTES

COOK TIME
15

SERVING
12

INGREDIENTS

- 9 eggs
- 1/2 cup onion, sliced
- 1 tbsp olive oil
- 8 oz ground sausage
- 1/4 cup coconut milk
- 1/2 tsp oregano
- 1 1/2 cups spinach
- 3/4 cup bell peppers, chopped
- Pepper
- Salt

DIRECTIONS

1. Preheat the air fryer to 325 F.
2. Add ground sausage in a pan and sauté over medium heat for 5 minutes
3. Add olive oil, oregano, bell pepper, and onion and sauté until onion is translucent.
4. Put spinach to the pan and cook for 30 seconds.
5. Remove pan from heat and set aside.
6. In a mixing bowl, whisk together eggs, coconut milk, pepper, and salt until well beaten.
7. Add sausage and vegetable mixture into the egg mixture and mix well.
8. Pour egg mixture into the silicone muffin molds and place into the air fryer basket. (Cook in batches)
9. Cook muffins for 15 minutes
10. Serve and enjoy.

Nutrition: Calories 135, Fat 11 g, Carbs 1.5 g, Protein 8 g

29. BLUEBERRY BREAKFAST COBBLER

PREPARATION TIME
5 MINUTES

COOK TIME
15

SERVING
4

INGREDIENTS

- ⅓ cup whole-wheat pastry flour
- ¾ teaspoon baking powder
- Dash sea salt
- ½ cup 2% milk
- 2 tablespoons pure maple syrup
- ½ teaspoon vanilla extract
- Cooking oil spray
- ½ cup fresh blueberries
- ¼ cup Granola, or plain store-bought granola

DIRECTIONS

1. In a medium bowl, whisk the flour, baking powder, and salt. Add the milk, maple syrup, and vanilla and gently whisk, just until thoroughly combined.
2. Preheat the unit by selecting BAKE, setting the temperature to 350°F, and setting the time to 3 minutes Select START/STOP to start.
3. Spray a 6-by-2-inch round baking pan with cooking oil and pour the batter into the pan. Top evenly with the blueberries and granola.
4. Once the unit is preheated, place the pan into the basket.
5. Select BAKE, set the temperature to 350°F, and set the time to 15 minutes Select START/STOP to begin.
6. When the cooking is complete, the cobbler should be nicely browned and a knife inserted into the middle should come out clean. Enjoy plain or topped with a little vanilla yogurt.

Nutrition: Calories 112, Fat 1g, Carbs 23g, Protein 3g

30. YUMMY BREAKFAST ITALIAN FRITTATA

PREPARATION TIME
5 MINUTES

COOK TIME
10

SERVING
6

INGREDIENTS

- 6 eggs
- 1/3 cup of milk
- 4-ounces of chopped Italian sausage
- 3 cups of stemmed and roughly chopped kale
- 1 red deseeded and chopped bell pepper
- ½ cup of a grated feta cheese
- 1 chopped zucchini
- 1 tablespoon of freshly chopped basil
- 1 teaspoon of garlic powder
- 1 teaspoon of onion powder
- 1 teaspoon of salt
- 1 teaspoon of black pepper

DIRECTIONS

1. Turn on your air fryer to 360 degrees Fahrenheit.
2. Grease the air fryer pan with a nonstick cooking spray.
3. Add the Italian sausage to the pan and cook it inside your air fryer for 5 minutes
4. While doing that, add and stir in the remaining ingredients until it mixes properly.
5. Add the egg mixture to the pan and allow it to cook inside your air fryer for 5 minutes
6. Thereafter carefully remove the pan and allow it to cool off until it gets chill enough to serve.
7. Serve and enjoy!

Nutrition: Calories 225, Fat 14g, Carbs 4.5g, Protein 20g

31. SAVORY CHEESE AND BACON MUFFINS

PREPARATION TIME
5 MINUTES

COOK TIME
17

SERVING
4

INGREDIENTS

- 1 ½ cup of all-purpose flour
- 2 teaspoons of baking powder
- ½ cup of milk
- 2 eggs
- 1 tablespoon of freshly chopped parsley
- 4 cooked and chopped bacon slices
- 1 thinly chopped onion
- ½ cup of shredded cheddar cheese
- ½ teaspoon of onion powder
- 1 teaspoon of salt
- 1 teaspoon of black pepper

DIRECTIONS

1. Turn on your air fryer to 360 degrees Fahrenheit.
2. Using a large bowl, add and stir all the ingredients until it mixes properly.
3. Then grease the muffin cups with a nonstick cooking spray or line it with a parchment paper. Pour the batter proportionally into each muffin cup.
4. Place it inside your air fryer and bake it for 15 minutes
5. Thereafter, carefully remove it from your air fryer and allow it to chill.
6. Serve and enjoy!

Nutrition: Calories 180, Fat 18g, Carbs 16g, Protein 15g

32. BEST AIR-FRIED ENGLISH BREAKFAST

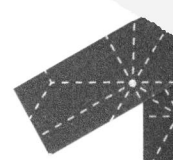

PREPARATION TIME
5 MINUTES

COOK TIME
20

SERVING
4

INGREDIENTS

- 8 sausages
- 8 bacon slices
- 4 eggs
- 1 (16-ounce) can of baked beans
- 8 slices of toast

DIRECTIONS

1. Add the sausages and bacon slices to your air fryer and cook them for 10 minutes at a 320 degrees Fahrenheit.
2. Using a ramekin or heat-safe bowl, add the baked beans, then place another ramekin and add the eggs and whisk.
3. Increase the temperature to 290 degrees Fahrenheit.
4. Place it inside your air fryer and cook it for an additional 10 minutes or until everything is done.
5. Serve and enjoy!

Nutrition: Calories 850, Fat 40g, Carbs 20g, Protein 48g

33. SAUSAGE AND EGG BREAKFAST BURRITO

PREPARATION TIME 5 MINUTES
COOK TIME 30
SERVING 6

INGREDIENTS

- 6 eggs
- Salt
- Pepper
- Cooking oil
- ½ cup chopped red bell pepper
- ½ cup chopped green bell pepper
- 8 ounces ground chicken sausage
- ½ cup salsa
- 6 medium (8-inch) flour tortillas
- ½ cup shredded Cheddar cheese

DIRECTIONS

1. In a medium bowl, whisk the eggs. Add salt and pepper to taste.
2. Place a skillet on medium-high heat. Spray with cooking oil. Add the eggs. Scramble for 2 to 3 minutes, until the eggs are fluffy. Remove the eggs from the skillet and set aside.
3. If needed, spray the skillet with more oil. Add the chopped red and green bell peppers. Cook for 2 to 3 minutes, once the peppers are soft.
4. Add the ground sausage to the skillet. Break the sausage into smaller pieces using a spatula or spoon. Cook for 3 to 4 minutes, until the sausage is brown.
5. Add the salsa and scrambled eggs. Stir to combine. Remove the skillet from heat.
6. Spoon the mixture evenly onto the tortillas.
7. To form the burritos, fold the sides of each tortilla in toward the middle and then roll up from the bottom. You can secure each burrito with a toothpick. Or you can moisten the outside edge of the tortilla with a small amount of water. I prefer to use a cooking brush, but you can also dab with your fingers.
8. Spray the burritos with cooking oil and place them in the air fryer. Do not stack. Cook the burritos in batches if they do not all fit in the basket. Cook for 8 minutes
9. Open the air fryer and flip the burritos. Heat it for an additional 2 minutes or until crisp.
10. If necessary, repeat steps 8 and 9 for the remaining burritos.
11. Sprinkle the Cheddar cheese over the burritos. Cool before serving.

Nutrition: Calories 236, Fat 13g, Carbs 16g, Protein 15g

34. FRENCH TOAST STICKS

PREPARATION TIME
5 MINUTES

COOK TIME
15

SERVING
12

INGREDIENTS

- 4 slices Texas toast (or any thick bread, such as challah)
- 1 tablespoon butter
- 1 egg
- 1 teaspoon stevia
- 1 teaspoon ground cinnamon
- ¼ cup milk
- 1 teaspoon vanilla extract
- Cooking oil

DIRECTIONS

1. Cut each slice of bread into 3 pieces (for 12 sticks total).
2. Place the butter in a small, microwave-safe bowl. Heat for 15 seconds, or until the butter has melted.
3. Remove the bowl from the microwave. Add the egg, stevia, cinnamon, milk, and vanilla extract. Whisk until fully combined.
4. Sprinkle the air fryer basket with cooking oil.
5. Dredge each of the bread sticks in the egg mixture.
6. Place the French toast sticks in the air fryer. It is okay to stack them. Spray the French toast sticks with cooking oil. Cook for 8 minutes
7. Open the air fryer and flip each of the French toast sticks. Cook for an additional 4 minutes, or until the French toast sticks are crisp.
8. Cool before serving.

Nutrition: Calories 52, Fat 2g, Carbs 7g, Protein 2g

35. HOME-FRIED POTATOES

PREPARATION TIME
5 MINUTES

COOK TIME
25

SERVING
4

INGREDIENTS

- 3 large russet potatoes
- 1 tablespoon canola oil
- 1 tablespoon extra-virgin olive oil
- 1 teaspoon paprika
- Salt
- Pepper
- 1 cup chopped onion
- 1 cup chopped red bell pepper
- 1 cup chopped green bell pepper

DIRECTIONS

1. Cut the potatoes into ½-inch cubes. Place the potatoes in a large bowl of cold water and allow them to soak for at least 30 minutes, preferably an hour.
2. Dry out the potatoes and wipe thoroughly with paper towels. Return them to the empty bowl.
3. Add the canola and olive oils, paprika, and salt and pepper to flavor. Toss to coat the potatoes fully.
4. Transfer the potatoes to the air fryer. Cook for 20 minutes, shaking the air fryer basket every 5 minutes (a total of 4 times).
5. Put the onion and red and green bell peppers to the air fryer basket. Fry for an additional 3 to 4 minutes, or until the potatoes are cooked through and the peppers are soft.
6. Cool before serving.

Nutrition: Calories 279, Fat 8g, Carbs 50g, Protein 6g

36. HOMEMADE CHERRY BREAKFAST TARTS

PREPARATION TIME
15 MINUTES

COOK TIME
20

SERVING
6

INGREDIENTS

For the tarts:
- 2 refrigerated piecrusts
- ⅓ Cup cherry preserves
- 1 teaspoon cornstarch
- Cooking oil

For the frosting:
- ½ cup vanilla yogurt
- 1-ounce cream cheese
- 1 teaspoon stevia
- Rainbow sprinkles

DIRECTIONS

1. To make the tarts:
2. Place the piecrusts on a flat surface. Make use of a knife or pizza cutter, cut each piecrust into 3 rectangles, for 6 in total. (I discard the unused dough left from slicing the edges.)
3. In a small bowl, combine the preserves and cornstarch. Mix well.
4. Scoop 1 tablespoon of the preserve mixture onto the top half of each piece of piecrust.
5. Fold the bottom of each piece up to close the tart. Press along the edges of each tart to seal using the back of a fork.
6. Sprinkle the breakfast tarts with cooking oil and place them in the air fryer. I do not recommend piling the breakfast tarts. They will stick together if piled. You may need to prepare them in two batches. Cook for 10 minutes
7. Allow the breakfast tarts to cool fully before removing from the air fryer.
8. If needed, repeat steps 5 and 6 for the remaining breakfast tarts.
9. To make the frosting:
10. In a small bowl, mix the yogurt, cream cheese, and stevia. Mix well.
11. Spread the breakfast tarts with frosting and top with sprinkles, and serve.

Nutrition: Calories 119, Fat 4g, Carbs 19g, Protein 2g

37. SAUSAGE AND CREAM CHEESE BISCUITS

PREPARATION TIME
5 MINUTES

COOK TIME
15

SERVING
5

INGREDIENTS

- 12 ounces chicken breakfast sausage
- 1 (6-ounce) can biscuits
- ⅛ cup cream cheese

DIRECTIONS

1. Form the sausage into 5 small patties.
2. Place the sausage patties in the air fryer. Cook for 5 minutes
3. Open the air fryer. Flip the patties. Cook for an additional 5 minutes
4. Remove the cooked sausages from the air fryer.
5. Separate the biscuit dough into 5 biscuits.
6. Place the biscuits in the air fryer. Cook for 3 minutes
7. Open the air fryer. Flip the biscuits. Cook for an additional 2 minutes
8. Remove the cooked biscuits from the air fryer.
9. Split each biscuit in half. Spread 1 teaspoon of cream cheese onto the bottom of each biscuit. Top with a sausage patty and the other half of the biscuit, and serve.

Nutrition: Calories 24g, Fat 13g, Carbs 20g, Protein 9g

38. FRIED CHICKEN AND WAFFLES

PREPARATION TIME
10 MINUTES

COOK TIME
30

SERVING
4

INGREDIENTS

- 8 whole chicken wings
- 1 teaspoon garlic powder
- Chicken seasoning or rub
- Pepper
- ½ cup all-purpose flour
- Cooking oil
- 8 frozen waffles
- Maple syrup (optional)

DIRECTIONS

1. In a medium bowl, spice the chicken with the garlic powder and chicken seasoning and pepper to flavor.
2. Put the chicken to a sealable plastic bag and add the flour. Shake to coat the chicken thoroughly.
3. Sprinkle the air fryer basket with cooking oil.
4. With the use of tongs, put the chicken from the bag to the air fryer. It is okay to pile the chicken wings on top of each other. Sprinkle them with cooking oil. Heat for five minutes
5. Unlock the air fryer and shake the basket. Presume to cook the chicken. Keep shaking every 5 minutes until 20 minutes has passed and the chicken is completely cooked.
6. Take out the cooked chicken from the air fryer and set aside.
7. Wash the basket and base out with warm water. Put them back to the air fryer.
8. Ease the temperature of the air fryer to 370°F.
9. Put the frozen waffles in the air fryer. Do not pile. Depends on how big your air fryer is, you may need to cook the waffles in batches. Sprinkle the waffles with cooking oil. Cook for 6 minutes
10. If necessary, take out the cooked waffles from the air fryer, then repeat step 9 for the leftover waffles.
11. Serve the waffles with the chicken and a bit of maple syrup if desired.

Nutrition: Calories 461, Fat 22g, Carbs 45g, Protein 28g

4. POULTRY RECIPES

39. PERFECT CHICKEN BREASTS

PREPARATION TIME
10 MINUTES

COOK TIME
15

SERVING
4

INGREDIENTS

- 1 lb chicken breasts, skinless and boneless
- 1 tsp poultry seasoning
- tsp olive oil
- 1 tsp salt

DIRECTIONS

1. Drizzle oil on the chicken breasts and season with poultry seasoning and salt.
2. Place chicken breasts into the air fryer basket and cook at 360 F for 10 minutes. Flip chicken and cook for 5 minutes more.
3. Serve and enjoy.

Nutrition: Calories 237, Fat 10.8 g, Carbohydrates 0.3 g, Sugar 0 g, Protein 32.9 g, Cholesterol 101 mg

40. RANCH GARLIC CHICKEN WINGS

PREPARATION TIME 10 MINUTES

COOK TIME 25

SERVING 4

INGREDIENTS

- lbs. chicken wings
- garlic cloves, minced
- 1/4 cup butter, melted
- tbsp ranch seasoning mix

DIRECTIONS

1. Add chicken wings into the zip-lock bag.
2. Mix together butter, garlic, and ranch seasoning and pour over chicken wings. Seal bag shakes well and places in the refrigerator overnight.
3. Place marinated chicken wings into the air fryer basket and cook at 360 F for 20 minutes. Shake air fryer basket twice.
4. Turn temperature to 390 F and cook chicken wings for 5 minutes more.
5. Serve and enjoy.

Nutrition: Calories 552, Fat 28.3 g, Carbohydrates 1.3 g, Sugar 0.1 g, Protein 66 g, Cholesterol 232 mg

41. RANCH CHICKEN THIGHS

PREPARATION TIME 10 MINUTES

COOK TIME 23

SERVING 4

INGREDIENTS

- chicken thighs, bone-in & skin-on
- 1/2 tbsp ranch dressing mix

DIRECTIONS

1. Add chicken thighs into the mixing bowl and sprinkle with ranch dressing mix. Toss well to coat.
2. Spray chicken thighs with cooking spray and place into the air fryer basket.
3. Cook at 380 F for 23 minutes. Turn chicken halfway through.
4. Serve and enjoy.

Nutrition: Calories 558, Fat 21.7 g, Carbohydrates 0.5 g, Sugar 0.3 g, Protein 84.6 g, Cholesterol 260 mg

42. TACO RANCH CHICKEN WINGS

PREPARATION TIME
10 MINUTES

COOK TIME
30

SERVING
4

INGREDIENTS

- lbs. chicken wings
- 1 tsp ranch seasoning
- 1 1/2 tsp taco seasoning
- 1 tsp olive oil

DIRECTIONS

1. Preheat the air fryer to 400 F.
2. In a mixing bowl, add chicken wings, ranch seasoning, taco seasoning, and oil and toss well to coat.
3. Place chicken wings into the air fryer basket and cook for 15 minutes.
4. Turn chicken wings to another side and cook for 15 minutes more.
5. Serve and enjoy.

Nutrition: Calories 444, Fat 18 g, Carbohydrates 0 g, Sugar 0 g, Protein 65.6 g, Cholesterol 202 mg

43. SIMPLE CAJUN CHICKEN WINGS

PREPARATION TIME
10 MINUTES

COOK TIME
25

SERVING
4

INGREDIENTS

- lbs. chicken wings
- 1/3 cup ranch dressing
- 1 tbsp + 1/2 tsp Cajun seasoning

DIRECTIONS

1. Rub 1 tablespoon Cajun seasoning all over chicken wings.
2. Place chicken wings into the air fryer basket and cook at 400 F for 25 minutes. Turn chicken wings halfway through.
3. Meanwhile, in a small bowl, mix together ranch dressing and 1 teaspoon Cajun seasoning.
4. Serve chicken wings with Cajun ranch dressing.

Nutrition: Calories 437 Fat 16.9 g Carbohydrates 1.1 g Sugar 0.5 g Protein 65.9 g Cholesterol 202 mg

44. SIMPLE AIR FRIED CHICKEN

PREPARATION TIME
10 MINUTES

COOK TIME
10

SERVING
4

INGREDIENTS

- oz chicken, skinless and boneless
- 1/2 tsp black pepper
- 1/2 tsp salt
- 1/2 cup almond meal
- 1 egg, beaten

DIRECTIONS

1. Preheat the air fryer at 330 F/ 165 C.
2. Add egg in a bowl and whisk until frothy and season with pepper and salt.
3. In a shallow dish, mix together almond meal and salt.
4. Dip chicken into the egg mixture then coats with almond meal.
5. Place coated chicken into the air fryer basket and cook for 10 minutes.
6. Serve and enjoy.

Nutrition: Calories 285; Fat 12.8 g; Carbohydrates 3.7 g; Protein 38.1 g;

45. BUFFALO WINGS

PREPARATION TIME
5 MINUTES

COOK TIME
15

SERVING
4

INGREDIENTS

- 32 oz chicken wings
- 1/4 cup hot sauce
- tbsp grass-fed butter, melted
- Salt

DIRECTIONS

1. Add chicken wings into the bowl. Pour hot sauce and butter over chicken wings and toss well.
2. Place marinated chicken wings into the refrigerator for 1-2 hours.
3. Preheat the air fryer at 400 F/ 204 C for 3 minutes
4. Place marinated chicken wings into the air fryer basket and cook for 12 minutes. shake basket halfway through.
5. Serve and enjoy.

Nutrition: Calories 678; Fat 34 g; Carbohydrates 0.4 g; Sugar 0.3 g; Protein 87.7 g; Cholesterol 300 mg

46. HONEY LIME CHICKEN WINGS

PREPARATION TIME
10 MINUTES

COOK TIME
50

SERVING
6

INGREDIENTS

- lbs chicken wings
- tbsp fresh lime juice
- salt and black pepper
- 1/4 tsp white pepper powder
- tbsp honey

DIRECTIONS

1. In a bowl, place all the ingredients and coat well.
2. Place marinated chicken wings into the refrigerator for 1-2 hours.
3. Preheat the air fryer to 182 C/ 360 F.
4. Place marinated chicken wings into the air fryer basket and cook for 12 minutes. Shake air fryer basket halfway through.
5. Turn temperature to 400 F/ 204 C and cook for 3 minutes more.
6. Serve and enjoy.

Nutrition: Calories 311; Fat 11.2 g; Carbohydrates 6.1 g; Sugar 5.8 g; Protein 43.8 g; Cholesterol 135 mg

47. SIMPLE CHICKEN DRUMSTICKS

PREPARATION TIME
10 MINUTES

COOK TIME
16

SERVING
4

INGREDIENTS

- 1 1/2 lbs chicken drumsticks
- tbsp chicken seasoning
- 1 tsp black pepper
- 1 tbsp olive oil
- 1 tsp salt

DIRECTIONS

1. In a small bowl, mix together chicken seasoning, olive oil, pepper, and salt.
2. Rub seasoning mixture all over the chicken.
3. Place seasoned chicken into the air fryer basket and cook for 10 minutes. Flip halfway through.
4. Turn temperature to 300 F/ 148 C and cook for 6 minutes more.
5. Serve and enjoy.

Nutrition: Calories 319; Fat 13.2 g; Carbohydrates 0.3 g; Sugar 0 g; Protein 46.8 g; Cholesterol 150 mg

48. HEALTHY CHICKEN WINGS

PREPARATION TIME
10 MINUTES

COOK TIME
25

SERVING
4

INGREDIENTS

- lbs. chicken wings
- 1 tbsp pepper
- 1 tbsp garlic powder
- tbsp seasoning salt

DIRECTIONS

1. In a bowl, mix all of the ingredients except for the chicken wings.
2. Add chicken wings in a bowl and toss until well coated.
3. Preheat the air fryer at 370 F/ 187 C for 5 minutes.
4. Put the chicken wings into the basket of the air fryer and cook for 20 minutes. Shake basket halfway through.
5. Serve and enjoy.

Nutrition: Calories 442; Fat 16.9 g; Carbohydrates 2.6 g; Sugar 0.5 g; Protein 66.1 g; Cholesterol 202 mg

49. THAI CHICKEN THIGHS

PREPARATION TIME 10 MINUTES

COOK TIME 20

SERVING 4

INGREDIENTS

- 1 lb chicken thighs, boneless and skinless
- tsp ginger, minced
- garlic cloves, chopped
- 1/2 cup coconut milk
- tbsp curry paste

DIRECTIONS

1. Add all ingredients into the zip-lock bag and shake well and place bag in the refrigerator for overnight.
2. Add marinated chicken and the sauce in a pie dish.
3. Place dish in air fryer and cook for 20 minutes at 165 F/ 73 C.
4. Serve and enjoy.

Nutrition: Calories 341; Fat 20 g; Carbohydrates 5.2 g; Sugar 1.1 g; Protein 34.1 g; Cholesterol 101 mg

50. CHICKEN PATTIES

PREPARATION TIME
10 MINUTES

COOK TIME
13

SERVING
8

INGREDIENTS

- lbs ground chicken
- 1 cup homemade salsa
- 1/2 small onion, chopped
- 1 1/2 cups egg whites
- Salt and Pepper

DIRECTIONS

1. Add egg whites, salsa, and onion into the blender and blend until combined.
2. Add ground chicken and egg mixture into the large mixing bowl. Season with pepper and salt and mix until well combined.
3. Make small patties from meat mixture.
4. Spray air fryer basket with cooking spray.
5. Place chicken patties in air fryer and cook for 12-13 minutes. Cook in batches.
6. Serve and enjoy.

Nutrition: Calories 357; Fat 12.7 g; Carbohydrates 2.8 g; Sugar 1.5 g; Protein 54.7 g; Cholesterol 151 mg

51. CAJUN SEASONED CHICKEN DRUMSTICKS

PREPARATION TIME
5 MINUTES

COOK TIME
15

SERVING
2

INGREDIENTS

- chicken drumsticks, skinless
- 1 tbsp Cajun seasoning
- tsp olive oil

DIRECTIONS

1. Add all ingredients to the zip-lock bag. Shake bag well and place in refrigerator for half hour.
2. Place marinated chicken drumsticks in air fryer basket and cook for 15 minutes at 400 F/ 204 C.
3. Serve and enjoy.

Nutrition: Calories 118; Fat 7.3 g; Carbohydrates 0 g; Sugar 0 g; Protein 12.7 g; Cholesterol 40 mg

52. HONEY GARLIC CHICKEN

PREPARATION TIME
10 MINUTES

COOK TIME
15

SERVING
2

INGREDIENTS

- chicken drumsticks, skinless
- 1/2 tsp garlic, minced
- tsp honey
- tsp olive oil

DIRECTIONS

1. Put all of the ingredients to a bowl and mix until well coated.
2. Place chicken in refrigerator for half hour.
3. Place marinated chicken into the air fryer and cook for 15 minutes at 400 F/ 204 C.
4. Serve and enjoy.

Nutrition: Calories 140; Fat 7.3 g; Carbohydrates 6 g; Sugar 5.8 g; Protein 12.7 g;

53. SRIRACHA CHICKEN WINGS

PREPARATION TIME
10 MINUTES

COOK TIME
35

SERVING
2

INGREDIENTS

- 1 lb. chicken wings
- 1/2 lime juice
- 1 tbsp grass-fed butter
- tbsp sriracha sauce
- 1/4 cup honey

DIRECTIONS

1. Preheat the air fryer to 182 C/ 360 F.
2. Add chicken wings in air fryer basket and cook for 30 minutes.
3. Meanwhile, in a pan, add all remaining ingredients and bring to boil for 3 minutes.
4. Once chicken wings are done then toss with sauce and serve.

Nutrition: Calories 711; Fat 32.6 g; Carbohydrates 35.9 g; Sugar 35.8 g; Protein 65.8 g; Cholesterol 227 mg

54. SWEET & SPICY CHICKEN WINGS

PREPARATION TIME
10 MINUTES

COOK TIME
20

SERVING
8

INGREDIENTS

- lbs. chicken wings
- tbsp honey
- 1/2 cup buffalo sauce
- tbsp grass-fed butter, melted
- Salt and Pepper

DIRECTIONS

1. Put the chicken wings into the basket of the air fryer and cook for 20 minutes at 400 F/ 204 C. Shake air fryer basket 2 times during the cooking.
2. In a large bowl, combine together honey, buffalo sauce, butter, pepper, and salt.
3. Add cooked chicken wings into the bowl and toss until well coated with sauce.
4. Serve and enjoy.

Nutrition: Calories 262; Fat 11.7 g; Carbohydrates 4.6 g; Sugar 4.4 g; Protein 32.9 g; Cholesterol 109 mg

55. GINGER GARLIC CHICKEN

PREPARATION TIME
10 MINUTES

COOK TIME
30

SERVING
2

INGREDIENTS

- chicken thighs, skinless and boneless
- 1/2 tsp ground ginger
- 1 garlic clove, minced
- tbsp ketchup
- 1/2 cup honey

DIRECTIONS

1. Cut chicken thighs into the small pieces and place them into the air fryer basket and cook for 25 minutes at 390 F/ 198 C.
2. Meanwhile, in a pan heat together honey, ketchup, garlic, and ground ginger for 4-5 minutes.
3. Once the chicken is cooked then transfer into the mixing bowl.
4. Pour honey mixture over the chicken and toss until well coated.
5. Serve and enjoy.

Nutrition: Calories 554; Fat 16.3 g; Carbohydrates 37.2 g; Sugar 36.5 g; Protein 63.7 g; Cholesterol 195 mg

56. SALT AND PEPPER WINGS

PREPARATION TIME
5 MINUTES

COOK TIME
10

SERVING
4

INGREDIENTS

- 2 teaspoons salt
- 2 teaspoons fresh ground pepper
- 2 pounds chicken wings

DIRECTIONS

1. In a bowl, mix the salt and pepper.
2. Add the wings to the bowl and mix with your hands to coat every last one.
3. Put 8 to 10 wings in the air fryer basket that has been sprayed with nonstick cooking spray. Set for 350 degrees F (there is no need to preheat) and cook about 15 minutes, turning once at 7 minutes.
4. Repeat with rest of wings and serve hot.

Nutrition: Calories 342 Fat 14.8 g Carbohydrates 1 g Sugar 0 g Protein 49.2 g Cholesterol 146 mg

57. PARMESAN CHICKEN WINGS

PREPARATION TIME
10 MINUTES

COOK TIME
25

SERVING
4

INGREDIENTS

- 1 1/2 lbs. chicken wings
- 3/4 tbsp garlic powder
- 1/4 cup parmesan cheese, grated
- 2 tbsp arrowroot powder
- Salt and Pepper

DIRECTIONS

1. Preheat the air fryer to 380 F.
2. In a bowl, mix the garlic powder, parmesan cheese, arrowroot powder, pepper, and salt together. Add chicken wings and toss until well coated.
3. Put the chicken wings into the air fryer basket. Spray top of chicken wings with cooking spray.
4. Select chicken and press start. Shake air fryer basket halfway through.
5. Serve and enjoy.

Nutrition: Calories 386 Fat 15.3 g Carbohydrates 5.6 g Sugar 0.4 g Protein 53.5 g Cholesterol 160 mg

58. WESTERN CHICKEN WINGS

PREPARATION TIME
10 MINUTES

COOK TIME
15

SERVING
4

INGREDIENTS

- 2 lbs. chicken wings
- 1 tsp Herb de Provence
- 1 tsp paprika
- 1/2 cup parmesan cheese, grated
- Salt and Pepper

DIRECTIONS

1. Add cheese, paprika, herb de Provence, pepper, and salt into the large mixing bowl. Place the chicken wings into the bowl and toss well to coat.
2. Preheat the air fryer to 350 F.
3. Place the chicken wings into the air fryer basket. Spray top of chicken wings with cooking spray.
4. Cook chicken wings for 15 minutes. Turn chicken wings halfway through.
5. Serve and enjoy.

Nutrition: Calories 473 Fat 19.6 g Carbohydrates 0.8 g Sugar 0.1 g Protein 69.7 g Cholesterol 211 mg

59. PERFECT CHICKEN THIGHS DINNER

PREPARATION TIME 10 MINUTES

COOK TIME 15

SERVING 4

INGREDIENTS

- 4 chicken thighs, bone-in & skinless
- 1/4 tsp ground ginger
- 2 tsp paprika
- 2 tsp garlic powder
- salt and pepper

DIRECTIONS

1. Preheat the air fryer to 400 F.
2. In a bowl, mix ginger, paprika, garlic powder, pepper, and salt together and rub all over chicken thighs.
3. Spray chicken thighs with cooking spray.
4. Place chicken thighs into the air fryer basket and cook for 10 minutes.
5. Turn chicken thighs and cook for 5 minutes more.
6. Serve and enjoy.

Nutrition: Calories 286 Fat 11 g Carbohydrates 1.8 g Sugar 0.5 g Protein 42.7 g Cholesterol 130 mg

60. PERFECTLY SPICED CHICKEN TENDERS

PREPARATION TIME
10 MINUTES

COOK TIME
13

SERVING
4

INGREDIENTS

- 6 chicken tenders
- 1 tsp onion powder
- 1 tsp garlic powder
- 1 tsp paprika
- 1 tsp kosher salt

DIRECTIONS

1. Preheat the air fryer to 380 F.
2. In a bowl, mix onion powder, garlic powder, paprika, and salt together and rub all over chicken tenders.
3. Spray chicken tenders with cooking spray.
4. Place chicken tenders into the air fryer basket and cook for 13 minutes.
5. Serve and enjoy.

Nutrition: Calories 423 Fat 16.4 g Carbohydrates 1.5 g Sugar 0.5 g Protein 63.7 g Cholesterol 195 mg

61. CHICKEN MEATBALLS

PREPARATION TIME
5 MINUTES

COOK TIME
15

SERVING
2

INGREDIENTS

- ½ lb chicken breast
- 1 tbsp of garlic
- 1 tbsp of onion
- ½ chicken broth
- 1 tbsp of oatmeal, whole wheat flour or of your choice

DIRECTIONS

1. Place all of the ingredients in a food processor and beat well until well mixed and ground.
2. If you don't have a food processor, ask the butcher to grind it and then add the other ingredients, mixing well.
3. Make balls and place them in the Air Fryer basket.
4. Program the Air Fryer for 15 minutes at 400°F.
5. Half the time shake the basket so that the meatballs loosen and fry evenly.

Nutrition: Calories: 45 Carbohydrates: 1.94g Fat: 1.57g Protein: 5.43g Sugar: 0.41g Cholesterol: 23m

62. HOMEMADE BREADED NUGGET IN DORITOS

PREPARATION TIME
10 MINUTES

COOK TIME
15

SERVING
4

INGREDIENTS

- ½ lb. boneless, skinless chicken breast
- ¼ lb. Doritos snack
- 1 cup of wheat flour
- 1 egg
- Salt, garlic and black pepper to taste.

DIRECTIONS

1. Cut the chicken breast in the width direction, 1 to 1.5 cm thick, so that it is already shaped like pips.
2. Season with salt, garlic, black pepper to taste and some other seasonings if desired.
3. You can also season with those seasonings or powdered onion soup.
4. Put the Doritos snack in a food processor or blender and beat until everything is crumbled, but don't beat too much, you don't want flour.
5. Now bread, passing the pieces of chicken breast first in the wheat flour, then in the beaten eggs and finally in the Doritos, without leaving the excess flour, eggs or Doritos.
6. Place the seeds in the Air Fryer basket and program for 15 minutes at 400°F, and half the time they brown evenly.

Nutrition: Calories: 42 Carbohydrates: 1.65g Fat: 1.44g Protein: 5.29g Sugar: 0.1g Cholesterol: 20mg

63. CHICKEN BREAST

PREPARATION TIME
30 MINUTES

COOK TIME
25

SERVING
6

INGREDIENTS

- 1 lb. diced clean chicken breast
- ½ lemon
- Smoked paprika to taste
- Black pepper or chili powder, to taste
- Salt to taste

DIRECTIONS

1. Flavor the chicken with salt, paprika and pepper and marinate.
2. Store in Air fryer and turn on for 15 minutes at 350°F.
3. Turn the chicken over and raise the temperature to 200°C, and turn the Air Fryer on for another 5 minutes or until golden.
4. Serve immediately.

Nutrition: Calories: 124 Carbohydrates: 0g Fat: 1.4g Protein: 26.1g Sugar: 0g Cholesterol: 66mg

64. BREADED CHICKEN WITHOUT FLOUR

PREPARATION TIME
10 MINUTES

COOK TIME
15

SERVING
6

INGREDIENTS

- 1 1/6 oz. of grated parmesan cheese
- 1 unit of egg
- 1 lb of chicken (breast)
- Salt and black pepper to taste

DIRECTIONS

1. Cut the chicken breast into 6 fillets and season with a little salt and pepper.
2. Beat the egg in a bowl.
3. Pass the chicken breast in the egg and then in the grated cheese, sprinkling the fillets.
4. Non-stick and put in the air fryer at 4000F for about 30 minutes or until golden brown.

Nutrition: Calories: 114 Carbohydrates: 13g Fat: 5.9g Protein: 2.3g Sugar: 3.2g Cholesterol: 19mg

65. BARBECUE WITH CHORIZO AND CHICKEN

PREPARATION TIME
5 MINUTES

COOK TIME
35

SERVING
4

INGREDIENTS

- 4 chicken thighs
- 2 Tuscan sausages
- 4 small onions

DIRECTIONS

1. Preheat the fryer to 400°F for 5 minutes. Season the meat the same way you would if you were going to use the barbecue.
2. Put in the fryer, lower the temperature to 160°C and set for 30 minutes.
3. After 20 minutes, check if any of the meat has reached the point of your preference. If so, take whichever is ready and return to the fryer with the others for another 10 minutes, now at 400°F. If not, return them to Air Fryer for the last 10 minutes at 400°F.

Nutrition: Calories: 135 Carbohydrates: 0g Fat: 5g Protein: 6g Sugar: 0g Cholesterol: 300mg

66. ROASTED THIGH

PREPARATION TIME
5 MINUTES

COOK TIME
30

SERVING
1

INGREDIENTS

- 3 chicken thighs and thighs
- 2 red seasonal bags
- 1 clove garlic
- ½ tsp of salt
- 1 pinch of black pepper

DIRECTIONS

1. Season chicken with red season, minced garlic, salt, and pepper. Leave to act for 5-10 minutes to obtain the flavor.
2. Put the chicken in the basket of the air fryer and bake at 390°F for 20 minutes.
3. After that time, remove the Air Fryer basket and check the chicken spot. If it is still raw or not golden enough, turn it over and leave it for another 10 minutes at 350°F.
4. After the previous step, your chicken will be ready on the Air Fryer! Serve with doré potatoes and leaf salad.

Nutrition: Calories: 278 Carbohydrates: 0.1g Fat: 18g Protein: 31g Sugar: 0g Cholesterol: 166mg

67. COXINHA FIT

PREPARATION TIME
10 MINUTES

COOK TIME
10-15

SERVING
4

INGREDIENTS

- ½ lb. seasoned and minced chicken
- 1 cup light cottage cheese
- 1 egg
- Condiments to taste
- Flaxseed or oatmeal

DIRECTIONS

1. In a bowl, mix all of the ingredients together except flour.
2. Knead well with your hands and mold into coxinha format.
3. If you prefer you can fill it, add chicken or cheese.
4. Repeat the process until all the dough is gone.
5. Pass the drumsticks in the flour and put them in the fryer.
6. Bake for 10 to 15 minutes at 390°F or until golden. Now it only works!

Nutrition: Calories: 220 Carbohydrates: 40g Fat: 18g Protein: 100g Sugar: 5g Cholesterol: 3000mg

68. ROLLED TURKEY BREAST

PREPARATION TIME
5 MINUTES

COOK TIME
10

SERVING
4

INGREDIENTS

- 1 box of cherry tomatoes
- ¼ lb. turkey blanket

DIRECTIONS

1. Wrap the turkey and blanket in the tomatoes, close with the help of toothpicks.
2. Take to Air Fryer for 10 minutes at 3900F.
3. You can increase the filling with ricotta and other preferred light ingredients.

Nutrition: Calories: 172 Carbohydrates: 3g Fat: 2g Protein: 34g Sugar: 1g Cholesterol: 300mg

69. CHICKEN IN BEER

PREPARATION TIME
5 MINUTES

COOK TIME
10

SERVING
4

INGREDIENTS

- 2 ¼ lbs chicken thigh and thigh
- ½ can of beer
- 4 cloves of garlic
- 1 large onion
- Pepper and salt to taste

DIRECTIONS

1. Wash the chicken pieces and, if desired, remove the skin to be healthier.
2. Place on an ovenproof plate.
3. In the blender, beat the other ingredients: beer, onion, garlic, and add salt and pepper, all together.
4. Cover the chicken with this mixture; it has to stay like swimming in the beer.
5. Take to the preheated air fryer at 3900F for 45 minutes.
6. It will roast when it has a brown cone on top and the beer has dried a bit.

Nutrition: Calories: 674 Carbohydrates: 5.47g Fat: 41.94g Protein: 61.94g Sugar: 1.62g Cholesterol: 206mg

70. CHICKEN FILLET

PREPARATION TIME
5 MINUTES

COOK TIME
20

SERVING
4

INGREDIENTS

- 4 chicken fillets
- salt to taste
- 1 garlic clove, crushed
- thyme to taste
- black pepper to taste

DIRECTIONS

1. Add seasoning to fillets, wrapping well for flavor. Heat up the Air Fryer for 5 minutes at 350°F. Place the fillets in the basket, program for 20 minutes at 350°F.
2. With 5 minutes remaining, turn the fillets and raise the temperature to 3900F. Serve!

Nutrition: Calories: 90 Carbohydrates:1g Fat: 1g Protein: 17g Sugar: 0g Cholesterol: 45mg

71. CHICKEN WITH LEMON AND BAHIAN SEASONING

PREPARATION TIME
2 HOURS

COOK TIME
20

SERVING
4

INGREDIENTS

- 5 pieces of chicken to bird;
- 2 garlic cloves, crushed;
- 4 tablespoons of lemon juice;
- 1 coffee spoon of Bahian spices;
- salt and black pepper to taste.

DIRECTIONS

1. Place the chicken pieces in a covered bowl and add the spices. Add the lemon juice. Cover the container and let the chicken marinate for 2 hours.
2. Place each piece of chicken in the basket of the air fryer, without overlapping the pieces. Set the fryer for 20 minutes at 390°F. In half the time, brown evenly. Serve!

Nutrition: Calories: 316.2 Carbohydrates: 4.9g Fat: 15.3g Protein: 32.8g Sugar: 0g

72. BASIC BBQ CHICKEN

PREPARATION TIME
5 MINUTES

COOK TIME
20

SERVING
4

INGREDIENTS

- 2 tablespoons Worcestershire Sauce
- 1 tablespoon honey
- ¾ cup ketchup
- 2 teaspoons chipotle chili powder
- 6 chicken drumsticks

DIRECTIONS

1. Heat up the air fryer to 370 degrees F for 5 minutes.
2. Use a big bowl to mix the Worcestershire sauce, honey, ketchup and chili powder. Whisk it up well.
3. Drop in the drumsticks and turn them so they are all coated with the mixture.
4. Grease the basket of the air fryer with nonstick spray and place 3 chicken drumsticks in.
5. Cook for 17 minutes for large drumsticks 15 minutes for smaller ones, flipping when it reaches half the time.
6. Repeat with the other three drumsticks.

Nutrition: Calories: 145 Carbohydrates: 4.5g Fat: 2.6g Protein: 13g

73. BASIC NO FRILLS TURKEY BREAST

PREPARATION TIME
5 MINUTES

COOK TIME
50

SERVING
4

INGREDIENTS

- 1 bone in turkey breast (about 8 pounds)
- 2 tablespoons olive oil
- 2 tablespoons sea salt
- 1 tablespoon black pepper

DIRECTIONS

1. Warm up the air fryer to 360°F for about 8 minutes.
2. Rub the washed turkey breast with the olive oil both on the skin and on the inside of the cavity.
3. Sprinkle on the sea salt and black pepper.
4. Remove the basket from the air fryer and spray with butter or olive oil flavored nonstick spray.
5. Put the turkey in with the breast side down.
6. Cook 20 minutes and carefully turn the breast over.
7. Spray with cooking oil and cook another 20 minutes.
8. When done test with thermometer and it should read 165 degrees F. If not, put it back in for a few minutes.
9. Let the breast rest at least 15 minutes before cutting and serving.

Nutrition: Calories: 375 Carbohydrates: 8.2g Fat: 6.8g Protein: 15g

74. FAIRE-WORTHY TURKEY LEGS

PREPARATION TIME
5 MINUTES

COOK TIME
10

SERVING
4

INGREDIENTS

- 1 turkey leg
- 1 teaspoon olive oil
- 1 teaspoon poultry seasoning
- 1 teaspoon garlic powder
- salt and black pepper to taste

DIRECTIONS

1. Warm up the air fryer to 350°F for about 4 minutes.
2. Coat the leg with the olive oil. Just use your hands and rub it in.
3. In a small bowl, mix the poultry seasoning, garlic powder, salt and pepper. Rub it on the turkey leg.
4. Coat the inside of the air fryer basket with nonstick spray and place the turkey leg in.
5. Cook for 27 minutes, turning at 14 minutes. Be sure the leg is done by inserting a meat thermometer in the fleshy part of the leg and it should read 165 degrees F.

Nutrition: Calories: 325 Carbohydrates: 8.3g Fat: 10g Protein: 18g

75. HERB AIR FRIED CHICKEN THIGHS

PREPARATION TIME
5 MINUTES

COOK TIME
50

SERVING
4

INGREDIENTS

- 2 pounds deboned chicken thighs
- 1 teaspoon rosemary
- 1 teaspoon thyme
- 1 teaspoon garlic powder
- 1 large lemon

DIRECTIONS

1. Trim fat from thighs and salt and pepper all sides.
2. In a bowl, combine the rosemary, thyme, and garlic powder. Sprinkle over the chicken thighs and press the mixture in putting them on a baking sheet.
3. Cut the lemon and squeeze the juice over all the chicken thighs. Cover with plastic wrap and put in the refrigerator for 30 minutes.
4. Warm up the air fryer to 360 degrees F for 6 minutes and spray with butter flavored cooking spray.
5. Place the thighs in the air fryer basket, as many will fit in one layer.
6. Cook for 15 minutes, turning after 7 minutes. Check internal temperature to make sure it is at 180 degrees F before serving.

Nutrition: Calories 534 Fat 27.8 g Carbohydrates 2.5 g Sugar 0.5 g Protein 66.2 g Cholesterol 202 mg

76. QUICK & EASY LEMON PEPPER CHICKEN

PREPARATION TIME 10 MINUTES

COOK TIME 30

SERVING 4

INGREDIENTS

- chicken breasts, boneless & skinless
- 1 1/2 tsp granulated garlic
- 1 tbsp lemon pepper seasoning
- 1 tsp salt

DIRECTIONS

1. Preheat the air fryer to 360 F.
2. Season chicken breasts with lemon pepper seasoning, granulated garlic, and salt.
3. Place chicken into the air fryer basket and cook for 30 minutes. Turn chicken halfway through.
4. Serve and enjoy.

Nutrition: Calories 285 Fat 10.9 g Carbohydrates 1.8 g Sugar 0.3 g Protein 42.6 g Cholesterol 130 mg

77. SPICY JALAPENO HASSEL BACK CHICKEN

PREPARATION TIME 10 MINUTES

COOK TIME 15

SERVING 2

INGREDIENTS

- chicken breasts, boneless and skinless
- 1/2 cup cheddar cheese, shredded
- tbsp pickled jalapenos, chopped
- oz cream cheese, softened
- bacon slices, cooked and crumbled

DIRECTIONS

1. Make five to six slits on top of chicken breasts.
2. In a bowl, mix together 1/2 cheddar cheese, pickled jalapenos, cream cheese, and bacon.
3. Stuff cheddar cheese mixture into the slits.
4. Place chicken into the air fryer basket and cook at 350 F for 14 minutes.
5. Sprinkle remaining cheese on top of the chicken and air fry for 1 minute more.
6. Serve and enjoy.

Nutrition: Calories 736 Fat 49 g Carbohydrates 3.7 g Sugar 0.2 g Protein 65.5 g Cholesterol 233 mg

78. TASTY HASSEL BACK CHICKEN

PREPARATION TIME
10 MINUTES

COOK TIME
18

SERVING
2

INGREDIENTS

- chicken breasts, boneless and skinless
- 1/2 cup sauerkraut, squeezed and remove excess liquid
- thin Swiss cheese slices, tear into pieces
- thin deli corned beef slices, tear into pieces
- Salt and Pepper

DIRECTIONS

1. Make five slits on top of chicken breasts. Season chicken with pepper and salt.
2. Stuff each slit with beef, sauerkraut, and cheese.
3. Spray chicken with cooking spray and place in the air fryer basket.
4. Cook chicken at 350 F for 18 minutes.
5. Serve and enjoy.

Nutrition: Calories 724 Fat 39.9 g Carbohydrates 3.6 g Sugar 2.6 g Protein 83.6 g Cholesterol 260 mg

79. WESTERN TURKEY BREAST

PREPARATION TIME
10 MINUTES

COOK TIME
60

SERVING
8

INGREDIENTS

- lbs. turkey breast, boneless
- 1 tbsp olive oil
- 1 1/2 tsp paprika
- 1 1/2 tsp garlic powder
- Salt and pepper

DIRECTIONS

1. Preheat the air fryer to 350 F.
2. In a bowl, mix paprika, garlic powder, pepper, and salt together.
3. Rub oil and spice mixture all over turkey breast.
4. Place turkey breast skin side down in the air fryer basket and cook for 25 minutes.
5. Turn turkey breast and cover with foil and cook for 35-45 minutes more or until the internal temperature of the turkey reaches 160 F.
6. Remove turkey breast from the air fryer and allow it to cool for 10 minutes.
7. Slice and serve.

Nutrition: Calories 254 Fat 5.6 g Carbohydrates 10.4 g Sugar 8.1 g Protein 38.9 g Cholesterol 98 mg

80. LEMON PEPPER TURKEY BREAST

PREPARATION TIME
10 MINUTES

COOK TIME
60

SERVING
6

INGREDIENTS

- lbs turkey breast, de-boned
- 1 tsp lemon pepper seasoning
- 1 tbsp Worcestershire sauce
- tbsp olive oil
- 1/2 tsp salt

DIRECTIONS

1. Add olive oil, Worcestershire sauce, lemon pepper seasoning, and salt into the zip-lock bag. Add turkey breast to the marinade and coat well and marinate for 1-2 hours.
2. Remove turkey breast from marinade and place it into the air fryer basket.
3. Cook at 350 F for 25 minutes. Turn turkey breast and cook for 35 minutes more or until the internal temperature of turkey breast reaches 165 F.
4. Slice and serve.

Nutrition: Calories 279 Fat 8.4 g Carbohydrates 10.3 g Sugar 8.5 g Protein 38.8 g Cholesterol 98 mg

81. TENDER TURKEY LEGS

PREPARATION TIME
10 MINUTES

COOK TIME
27

SERVING
4

INGREDIENTS

- turkey legs
- 1/4 tsp oregano
- 1/4 tsp rosemary
- 1 tbsp butter
- Salt and Pepper

DIRECTIONS

1. Season turkey legs with pepper and salt.
2. In a small bowl, mix together butter, oregano, and rosemary.
3. Rub the butter mixture all over turkey legs.
4. Preheat the air fryer to 350 F.
5. Place turkey legs into the air fryer basket and cook for 27 minutes.
6. Serve and enjoy.

Nutrition: Calories 182 Fat 9.9 g Carbohydrates 1.9 g Sugar 0.1 g Protein 20.2 g Cholesterol 68 mg

5. MEAT RECIPES

82. BULLET-PROOF BEEF ROAST

PREPARATION TIME
2 HOUR

COOK TIME
2 H 5'

SERVING
2

INGREDIENTS

- 1 cup of organic beef
- tbsp. olive oil
- pounds beef round roast
- Salt and pepper, to taste

DIRECTIONS

1. Place all of the ingredients in a resealable bag and let it marinate in the fridge for about two hours.
2. Fix the temperature to 400° F and preheat the air-fryer for 5 minutes.
3. Place the ingredients in the Ziploc bag in a baking tray that will fit the air-fryer.
4. Let it cook for 2 hours at a temperature of 400 F.
5. Serve while it is warm.

Nutrition: Calories: 280 Carbs: 13 g Fat: 15 g Protein: 26 g

83. PORK AND POTATOES

PREPARATION TIME	COOK TIME	SERVING
5 MINUTES	25	4

INGREDIENTS

- 2 cups creamer potatoes, rinsed and dried
- 2 teaspoons olive oil (see Tip)
- 1 (1-pound) pork tenderloin, cut into 1-inch cubes
- 1 onion, chopped
- 1 red bell pepper, chopped
- 2 garlic cloves, minced
- ½ teaspoon dried oregano
- 2 tablespoons low-sodium chicken broth

DIRECTIONS

1. In a medium bowl, toss the potatoes and olive oil to coat.
2. Transfer the potatoes to the air fryer basket. Roast for 15 minutes.
3. In a medium metal bowl, mix the potatoes, pork, onion, red bell pepper, garlic, and oregano.
4. Drizzle with the chicken broth. Put the bowl in the air fryer basket. Roast for about 10 minutes more, shaking the basket once during cooking, until the pork reaches at least 145°F on a meat thermometer and the potatoes are tender. Serve immediately.

Nutrition: Calories: 235 Fat: 5g Saturated Fat: 1g Protein: 26g Carbohydrates: 22g Sodium: 66mg Fiber: 3g Sugar: 4g

84. PORK AND FRUIT KEBABS

PREPARATION TIME
15 MINUTES

COOK TIME
9-12

SERVING
4

INGREDIENTS

- ⅓ cup apricot jam
- 2 tablespoons freshly squeezed lemon juice
- 2 teaspoons olive oil
- ½ teaspoon dried tarragon
- 1 (1-pound) pork tenderloin, cut into 1-inch cubes
- 4 plums, pitted and quartered (see Tip)
- 4 small apricots, pitted and halved (see Tip)

DIRECTIONS

1. In a large bowl, mix the jam, lemon juice, olive oil, and tarragon.
2. Add the pork and stir to coat. Let stand for 10 minutes at room temperature.
3. Alternating the items, thread the pork, plums, and apricots onto 4 metal skewers that fit into the air fryer. Brush with any remaining jam mixture. Discard any remaining marinade.
4. Grill the kebabs in the air fryer for 9 to 12 minutes, or until the pork reaches 145°F on a meat thermometer and the fruit is tender. Serve immediately.

Nutrition: Calories: 256, Fat; 5g Saturated Fat; 1g, Protein: 24g, Carbohydrates: 30g, Sodium: 60mg, Fiber: 2g, Sugar: 22g

85. STEAK AND VEGETABLE KEBABS

PREPARATION TIME
15 MINUTES

COOK TIME
5-7

SERVING
4

INGREDIENTS

- 2 tablespoons balsamic vinegar
- 2 teaspoons olive oil
- ½ teaspoon dried marjoram
- ⅛ teaspoon freshly ground black pepper
- ¾ pound round steak, cut into 1-inch pieces
- 1 red bell pepper, sliced
- 16 button mushrooms
- 1 cup cherry tomatoes

DIRECTIONS

1. In a medium bowl, stir together the balsamic vinegar, olive oil, marjoram, and black pepper.
2. Add the steak and stir to coat. Let stand for 10 minutes at room temperature.
3. Alternating items, thread the beef, red bell pepper, mushrooms, and tomatoes onto 8 bamboo (see Tip, here) or metal skewers that fit in the air fryer.
4. Grill in the air fryer for 5 to 7 minutes, or until the beef is browned and reaches at least 145°F on a meat thermometer. Serve immediately.

Nutrition: Calories: 194 Fat: 6g Saturated Fat: 2g Protein: 31g Carbohydrates: 7g Sodium: 53mg Fiber: 2g Sugar: 2g

86. SPICY GRILLED STEAK

PREPARATION TIME
7 MINUTES

COOK TIME
6-9

SERVING
4

INGREDIENTS

- 2 tablespoons low-sodium salsa
- 1 tablespoon minced chipotle pepper
- 1 tablespoon apple cider vinegar
- 1 teaspoon ground cumin
- ⅛ teaspoon freshly ground black pepper
- ⅛ teaspoon red pepper flakes
- ¾ pound sirloin tip steak, cut into 4 pieces and gently pounded to about ⅓ inch thick

DIRECTIONS

1. In a small bowl, thoroughly mix the salsa, chipotle pepper, cider vinegar, cumin, black pepper, and red pepper flakes. Rub this mixture into both sides of each steak piece. Let stand for 15 minutes at room temperature.
2. Grill the steaks in the air fryer, two at a time, for 6 to 9 minutes, or until they reach at least 145°F on a meat thermometer.
3. Remove the steaks to a clean plate and cover with aluminum foil to keep warm. Repeat with the remaining steaks.
4. Slice the steaks thinly against the grain and serve.

Nutrition: Calories: 160 Fat: 6g Saturated Fat: 3g Protein: 24g Carbohydrates: 1g Sodium: 87mg Fiber: 0g Sugar: 0g

87. GREEK VEGETABLE SKILLET

PREPARATION TIME
9 MINUTES

COOK TIME
10-19

SERVING
4

INGREDIENTS

- ½ pound 96 percent lean ground beef
- 2 medium tomatoes, chopped
- 1 onion, chopped
- 2 garlic cloves, minced
- 2 cups fresh baby spinach (see Tip)
- 2 tablespoons freshly squeezed lemon juice
- ⅓ cup low-sodium beef broth
- 2 tablespoons crumbled low-sodium feta cheese

DIRECTIONS

1. In a 6-by-2-inch metal pan, crumble the beef. Cook in the air fryer for 3 to 7 minutes, stirring once during cooking, until browned. Drain off any fat or liquid.
2. Add the tomatoes, onion, and garlic to the pan. Air-fry for 4 to 8 minutes more, or until the onion is tender.
3. Add the spinach, lemon juice, and beef broth. Air-fry for 2 to 4 minutes more, or until the spinach is wilted.
4. Sprinkle with the feta cheese and serve immediately

Nutrition: Calories: 97 Fat: 1g Saturated Fat: 1g Protein: 15g Carbohydrates: 5g Sodium: 123mg Fiber: 1g Sugar: 2g

88. LIGHT HERBED MEATBALLS

PREPARATION TIME
10 MINUTES

COOK TIME
12-17

SERVING
24

INGREDIENTS

- 1 medium onion, minced
- 2 garlic cloves, minced
- 1 teaspoon olive oil
- 1 slice low-sodium whole-wheat bread, crumbled
- 3 tablespoons 1 percent milk
- 1 teaspoon dried marjoram
- 1 teaspoon dried basil
- 1-pound 96 percent lean ground beef

DIRECTIONS

1. In a 6-by-2-inch pan, combine the onion, garlic, and olive oil. Air-fry for 2 to 4 minutes, or until the vegetables are crisp-tender.
2. Transfer the vegetables to a medium bowl, and add the bread crumbs, milk, marjoram, and basil. Mix well.
3. Add the ground beef. With your hands, work the mixture gently but thoroughly until combined. Form the meat mixture into about 24 (1-inch) meatballs.
4. Bake the meatballs, in batches, in the air fryer basket for 12 to 17 minutes, or until they reach 160°F on a meat thermometer. Serve immediately.

Nutrition: Calories: 190 Fat: 6g Saturated Fat: 2g Protein: 25g Carbohydrates: 8g Sodium: 120mg Fiber: 1g; Sugar: 2g 1% DV vitamin A 3% DV vitamin C

89. BROWN RICE AND BEEF-STUFFED BELL PEPPERS

PREPARATION TIME
10 MINUTES

COOK TIME
11-16

SERVING
4

INGREDIENTS

- 4 medium bell peppers, any colors, rinsed, tops removed
- 1 medium onion, chopped
- ½ cup grated carrot
- 2 teaspoons olive oil
- 2 medium beefsteak tomatoes, chopped
- 1 cup cooked brown rice
- 1 cup chopped cooked low-sodium roast beef (see Tip)
- 1 teaspoon dried marjoram

DIRECTIONS

1. Remove the stems from the bell pepper tops and chop the tops.
2. In a 6-by-2-inch pan, combine the chopped bell pepper tops, onion, carrot, and olive oil. Cook for 2 to 4 minutes, or until the vegetables are crisp-tender.
3. Transfer the vegetables to a medium bowl. Add the tomatoes, brown rice, roast beef, and marjoram. Stir to mix.
4. Stuff the vegetable mixture into the bell peppers. Place the bell peppers in the air fryer basket. Bake for 11 to 16 minutes, or until the peppers are tender and the filling is hot. Serve immediately.

Nutrition: Calories: 206 Fat: 6g Saturated Fat: 1g Protein: 18g Carbohydrates: 20g Sodium: 105mg Fiber: 3g Sugar: 5g

90. BEEF AND BROCCOLI

PREPARATION TIME
10 MINUTES

COOK TIME
14-18

SERVING
4

INGREDIENTS

- 2 tablespoons cornstarch
- ½ cup low-sodium beef broth
- 1 teaspoon low-sodium soy sauce
- 12 ounces sirloin strip steak, cut into 1-inch cubes
- 2½ cups broccoli florets
- 1 onion, chopped
- 1 cup sliced cremini mushrooms (see Tip)
- 1 tablespoon grated fresh ginger
- Brown rice, cooked (optional)

DIRECTIONS

1. In a medium bowl, stir together the cornstarch, beef broth, and soy sauce.
2. Add the beef and toss to coat. Let stand for 5 minutes at room temperature.
3. With a slotted spoon, transfer the beef from the broth mixture into a medium metal bowl. Reserve the broth.
4. Add the broccoli, onion, mushrooms, and ginger to the beef. Place the bowl into the air fryer and cook for 12 to 15 minutes, or until the beef reaches at least 145°F on a meat thermometer and the vegetables are tender.
5. Add the reserved broth and cook for 2 to 3 minutes more, or until the sauce boils.
6. Serve immediately over hot cooked brown rice, if desired.

Nutrition: Calories: 240 Fat: 6g Saturated Fat: 2g Protein: 19g Carbohydrates: 11g Sodium: 107mg Fiber: 2g Sugar: 3g

91. BEEF AND FRUIT STIR-FRY

PREPARATION TIME
15 MINUTES

COOK TIME
6-11

SERVING
4

INGREDIENTS

- 12 ounces sirloin tip steak, thinly sliced
- 1 tablespoon freshly squeezed lime juice
- 1 cup canned mandarin orange segments, drained, juice reserved (see Tip)
- 1 cup canned pineapple chunks, drained, juice reserved (see Tip)
- 1 teaspoon low-sodium soy sauce
- 1 tablespoon cornstarch
- 1 teaspoon olive oil
- 2 scallions, white and green parts, sliced
- Brown rice, cooked (optional)

DIRECTIONS

1. In a medium bowl, mix the steak with the lime juice. Set aside.
2. In a small bowl, thoroughly mix 3 tablespoons of reserved mandarin orange juice, 3 tablespoons of reserved pineapple juice, the soy sauce, and cornstarch.
3. Drain the beef and transfer it to a medium metal bowl, reserving the juice. Stir the reserved juice into the mandarin-pineapple juice mixture. Set aside.
4. Add the olive oil and scallions to the steak. Place the metal bowl in the air fryer and cook for 3 to 4 minutes, or until the steak is almost cooked, shaking the basket once during cooking.
5. Stir in the mandarin oranges, pineapple, and juice mixture. Cook for 3 to 7 minutes more, or until the sauce is bubbling and the beef is tender and reaches at least 145°F on a meat thermometer.
6. Stir and serve over hot cooked brown rice, if desired.

Nutrition: Calories: 212 Fat: 4g Saturated Fat: 1g Protein: 19g Carbohydrates: 28g Sodium: 105mg Fiber: 2g Sugar: 22g

92. GARLIC PUTTER PORK CHOPS

PREPARATION TIME
10 MINUTES

COOK TIME
10

SERVING
4

INGREDIENTS

- tsp. parsley
- tsp. grated garlic cloves
- 1 tbsp. coconut oil
- 1 tbsp. coconut butter
- pork chops

DIRECTIONS

1. Preparing the Ingredients. Ensure your air fryer is preheated to 350 degrees.
2. Mix butter, coconut oil, and all seasoning together. Then rub seasoning mixture over all sides of pork chops. Place in foil, seal, and chill for 1 hour.
3. Remove pork chops from foil and place into air fryer.
4. Air Frying. Set temperature to 350°F, and set time to 7 minutes. Cook 7 minutes on one side and 8 minutes on the other.
5. Drizzle with olive oil and serve alongside a green salad.

Nutrition: Calories: 526; Fat: 23g; Protein:41g; Sugar:4g

93. CAJUN PORK STEAKS

PREPARATION TIME
5 MINUTES

COOK TIME
20

SERVING
6

INGREDIENTS

- 4-6 pork steaks

BBQ sauce:
- Cajun seasoning
- 1 tbsp. vinegar
- 1 tsp. low-sodium soy sauce
- ½ C. brown sugar

DIRECTIONS

1. Preparing the Ingredients. Ensure your air fryer is preheated to 290 degrees.
2. Sprinkle pork steaks with Cajun seasoning.
3. Combine remaining ingredients and brush onto steaks. Add coated steaks to air fryer.
4. Air Frying. Set temperature to 290°F, and set time to 20 minutes. Cook 15-20 minutes till just browned.

Nutrition: Calories: 209; Fat: 11g; Protein:28g; Sugar:2g

94. CAJUN SWEET-SOUR GRILLED PORK

PREPARATION TIME 5 MINUTES

COOK TIME 12

SERVING 3

INGREDIENTS

- ¼ cup brown sugar
- 1/4 cup cider vinegar
- 1-lb pork loin, sliced into 1-inch cubes
- tablespoons Cajun seasoning
- tablespoons brown sugar

DIRECTIONS

1. Preparing the Ingredients. In a shallow dish, mix well pork loin, 3 tablespoons brown sugar, and Cajun seasoning. Toss well to coat. Marinate in the ref for 3 hours.
2. In a medium bowl mix well, brown sugar and vinegar for basting.
3. Thread pork pieces in skewers. Baste with sauce and place on skewer rack in air fryer.
4. Air Frying. For 12 minutes, cook on 360°F. Halfway through Cooking Time, turnover skewers and baste with sauce. If needed, cook in batches.
5. Serve and enjoy.

Nutrition: Calories: 428; Fat: 16.7g; Protein:39g; Sugar:2g

95. PORK LOIN WITH POTATOES

PREPARATION TIME
10 MINUTES

COOK TIME
25

SERVING
2

INGREDIENTS

- pounds pork loin
- large red potatoes, chopped
- ½ teaspoon garlic powder
- ½ teaspoon red pepper flakes, crushed
- Salt and black pepper, to taste

DIRECTIONS

1. In a large bowl, put all of the ingredients together except glaze and toss to coat well. Preheat the Air fryer to 325 degrees F. Place the loin in the air fryer basket.
2. Arrange the potatoes around pork loin.
3. Cook for about 25 minutes.

Nutrition: Calories:260 Fat: 8g Carbs: 27g Protein: 21g

96. ROASTED CHAR SIEW (PORK BUTT)

PREPARATION TIME 10 MINUTES
COOK TIME 25
SERVING 4

INGREDIENTS

- 1 strip of pork shoulder butt with a good amount of fat marbling

Marinade:
- 1 tsp. sesame oil
- tbsp. raw honey
- 1 tsp. light soy sauce
- 1 tbsp. rose wine

DIRECTIONS

1. Mix all of the marinade ingredients together and put it to a Ziploc bag. Place pork in bag, making sure all sections of pork strip are engulfed in the marinade. Chill 3-24 hours.
2. Take out the strip 30 minutes before planning to cook and preheat your air fryer to 350 degrees.
3. Place foil on small pan and brush with olive oil. Place marinated pork strip onto prepared pan.
4. Set temperature to 350°F, and set time to 20 minutes. Roast 20 minutes.
5. Glaze with marinade every 5-10 minutes.
6. Remove strip and leave to cool a few minutes before slicing.

Nutrition: Calories: 289; Fat: 13g; Protein:33g; Sugar:1g

97. ASIAN PORK CHOPS

PREPARATION TIME
2 HOUR 10'

COOK TIME
15

SERVING
2

INGREDIENTS

- 1/2 cup hoisin sauce
- tablespoons cider vinegar
- 1 tablespoon Asian sweet chili sauce
- (1/2-inch-thick) boneless pork chops
- salt and pepper

DIRECTIONS

1. Stir together hoisin, chili sauce, and vinegar in a large mixing bowl. Separate a quarter cup of this mixture, then add pork chops to the bowl and let it sit in the fridge for 2 hours. Take out the pork chops and place them on a plate. Sprinkle each side of the pork chop evenly with salt and pepper.
2. Cook at 360 degrees for 14 minutes, flipping half way through. Brush with reserved marinade and serve.

Nutrition: Calories: 338; Fat: 21g; Protein:19g; Fiber:1g

98. MARINATED PORK CHOPS

PREPARATION TIME
10 MINUTES

COOK TIME
30

SERVING
2

INGREDIENTS

- pork chops, boneless
- 1 tsp garlic powder
- ½ cup flour
- 1 cup buttermilk
- Salt and pepper

DIRECTIONS

1. Add pork chops and buttermilk in a zip-lock bag. Seal the bag and set aside in the refrigerator overnight.
2. In another zip-lock bag add flour, garlic powder, pepper, and salt.
3. Remove marinated pork chops from buttermilk and add in flour mixture and shake until well coated.
4. Preheat the instant vortex air fryer oven to 380 F.
5. Spray air fryer tray with cooking spray.
6. Arrange pork chops on a tray and air fryer for 28-30 minutes. Turn pork chops after 18 minutes.
7. Serve and enjoy.

Nutrition: Calories 424 Fat 21.3 g Carbs 30.8 g Protein 25.5 g

99. STEAK WITH CHEESE BUTTER

PREPARATION TIME
10 MINUTES

COOK TIME
8-10

SERVING
2

INGREDIENTS

- rib-eye steaks
- tsp garlic powder
- 1/2 tbsp blue cheese butter
- 1 tsp pepper
- tsp kosher salt

DIRECTIONS

1. Preheat the air fryer to 400 F.
2. Mix together garlic powder, pepper, and salt and rub over the steaks.
3. Spray air fryer basket with cooking spray.
4. Put the steak in the air fryer basket and cook for 4-5 minutes on each side.
5. Top with blue butter cheese.
6. Serve and enjoy.

Nutrition: Calories 830 Fat 60 g Carbohydrates 3 g Sugar 0 g Protein 70g Cholesterol 123 mg

100. MADEIRA BEEF

PREPARATION TIME
5 MINUTES

COOK TIME
25

SERVING
6

INGREDIENTS

- 1 cup Madeira
- 1 and ½ pounds beef meat, cubed
- Salt and black pepper to the taste
- 1 yellow onion, thinly sliced
- 1 chili pepper, sliced

DIRECTIONS

1. Put the reversible rack in the Air fryer, add the baking pan inside and mix all the ingredients in it.
2. Cook on Baking mode at 380 degrees F for 25 minutes, divide the mix into bowls and serve.

Nutrition: Calories 295, Fat 16, Fiber 9, Carbs 20, Protein 15.

101. CREAMY PORK AND ZUCCHINIS

PREPARATION TIME
5 MINUTES

COOK TIME
25

SERVING
4

INGREDIENTS

- 1 and ½ pounds pork stew meat, cubed
- 1 cup tomato sauce
- 1 tablespoon olive oil
- zucchinis, sliced
- Salt and black pepper to the taste

DIRECTIONS

1. Put the reversible rack in the Air fryer, add the baking pan inside and mix all the ingredients in it.
2. Cook on Baking mode at 380 degrees F, divide the mix into bowls and serve.

Nutrition: Calories 284, Fat 12, Fiber 9, Carbs 17, Protein 12.

102. JUICY STEAK BITES

PREPARATION TIME
10 MINUTES

COOK TIME
9

SERVING
4

INGREDIENTS

- 1 lb sirloin steak, sliced into bite-size pieces
- 1 tbsp steak seasoning
- 1 tbsp olive oil
- Pepper
- Salt

DIRECTIONS

1. Preheat the instant air fryer oven to 390 F.
2. Add steak pieces into the large mixing bowl. Add steak seasoning, oil, pepper, and salt over steak pieces and toss until well coated.
3. Transfer steak pieces on instant vortex air fryer pan and air fry for 5 minutes.
4. Turn steak pieces to the other side and cook for 4 minutes more.
5. Serve and enjoy.

Nutrition: Calories 241 Fat 10.6 g Carbohydrates 0 g Sugar 0 g Protein 34.4 g Cholesterol 101 mg

103. GREEK LAMB CHOPS

PREPARATION TIME
10 MINUTES

COOK TIME
10

SERVING
4

INGREDIENTS

- 2 lbs. lamb chops
- 2 tsp garlic, minced
- 1 ½ tsp dried oregano
- ¼ cup fresh lemon juice
- salt and pepper

DIRECTIONS

1. Add lamb chops in a mixing bowl. Add remaining ingredients over the lamb chops and coat well.
2. Arrange lamb chops on the air fryer oven tray and cook at 400 F for 5 minutes.
3. Turn lamb chops and cook for 5 minutes more.
4. Serve and enjoy.

Nutrition: Calories 538 Fat 29.4 g Carbohydrates 1.3 g Sugar 0.4 g Protein 64 g Cholesterol 204 mg

104. EASY BEEF ROAST

PREPARATION TIME
10 MINUTES

COOK TIME
45

SERVING
6

INGREDIENTS

- 2 ½ lbs. beef roast
- 2 tbsp Italian seasoning

DIRECTIONS

1. Arrange roast on the rotisserie spite.
2. Rub roast with Italian seasoning then insert into the instant vortex air fryer oven.
3. Air fry at 350 F for 45 minutes or until the internal temperature of the roast reaches to 145 F.
4. Slice and serve.

Nutrition: Calories 365 Fat 13.2 g Carbohydrates 0.5 g Sugar 0.4 g Protein 57.4 g Cholesterol 172 mg

105. BEEF JERKY

PREPARATION TIME
10 MINUTES

COOK TIME
4 H

SERVING
4

INGREDIENTS

- 2 lbs. London broil, sliced thinly
- 1 tsp onion powder
- 3 tbsp brown sugar
- 3 tbsp soy sauce
- 1 tsp olive oil

DIRECTIONS

1. Add all ingredients except meat in the large zip-lock bag.
2. Mix until well combined. Add meat in the bag.
3. Seal bag and massage gently to cover the meat with marinade.
4. Let marinate the meat for 1 hour.
5. Arrange marinated meat slices on instant vortex air fryer tray and dehydrate at 160 F for 4 hours.

Nutrition: Calories 133 Fat 4.7 g Carbohydrates 9.4 g Sugar 7.1 g Protein 13.4 g Cholesterol 0 mg

106. SIMPLE BEEF PATTIES

PREPARATION TIME
10 MINUTES

COOK TIME
13

SERVING
4

INGREDIENTS

- 1 lb. ground beef
- ½ tsp garlic powder
- ¼ tsp onion powder
- Pepper
- Salt

DIRECTIONS

1. Preheat the instant vortex air fryer oven to 400 F.
2. Add ground meat, garlic powder, onion powder, pepper, and salt into the mixing bowl and mix until well combined.
3. Make even shape patties from meat mixture and arrange on air fryer pan.
4. Place pan in instant vortex air fryer oven.
5. Cook patties for 10 minutes. Turn patties after 5 minutes.
6. Serve and enjoy.

Nutrition: Calories 212 Fat 7.1 g Carbohydrates 0.4 g Sugar 0.1 g Protein 34.5 g Cholesterol 101 mg

107. PORK TAQUITOS

PREPARATION TIME
10 MINUTES

COOK TIME
16

SERVING
8

INGREDIENTS

- 1 juiced lime
- 10 whole wheat tortillas
- 2 ½ c. Shredded mozzarella cheese
- 30 ounces of cooked and shredded pork tenderloin

DIRECTIONS

1. Preparing the ingredients. Ensure your air fryer is preheated to 380 degrees.
2. Drizzle pork with lime juice and gently mix.
3. Heat up tortillas in the microwave with a dampened paper towel to soften.
4. Add about 3 ounces of pork and ¼ cup of shredded cheese to each tortilla. Tightly roll them up.
5. Grease the air fryer basket with a drizzle of olive oil.
6. Air frying. Set temperature to 380°f, and set time to 10 minutes. Air fry taquitos 7-10 minutes till tortillas turn a slight golden color, making sure to flip halfway through cooking process.

Nutrition: Calories: 309; Fat: 11g; Protein:21g; Sugar:2g

108. PANKO-BREADED PORK CHOPS

PREPARATION TIME 5 MINUTES
COOK TIME 12
SERVING 6

INGREDIENTS

- 5 (3½- to 5-ounce) pork chops (bone-in or boneless)
- salt and pepper
- ¼ cup all-purpose flour
- 2 tablespoons panko bread crumbs
- Cooking oil

DIRECTIONS

1. Preparing the Ingredients. Season the pork chops with salt and pepper to taste.
2. Sprinkle the flour on both sides of the pork chops, then coat both sides with panko bread crumbs.
3. Put the pork chops in the air fryer. Stacking them is okay.
4. Air Frying. Spray the pork chops with cooking oil. Cook for 6 minutes.
5. Halfway through, flip the pork chops. Cook for an additional 6 minutes
6. Cool before serving.
7. Typically, bone-in pork chops are juicier than boneless. If you prefer really juicy pork chops, use bone-in.

Nutrition: Calories: 246; Fat: 13g; Protein:26g; Fiber:0g

109. CRISPY ROAST GARLIC-SALT PORK

PREPARATION TIME
5 MINUTES

COOK TIME
45

SERVING
4

INGREDIENTS

- 1 teaspoon Chinese five spice powder
- 1 teaspoon white pepper
- 2 pounds pork belly
- 2 teaspoons garlic salt

DIRECTIONS

1. Preparing the Ingredients. Preheat the air fryer to 390°F.
2. Mix all of the seasonings in a bowl to create the dry rub.
3. Score the skin of the pork belly with a knife and season the entire pork with the spice rub.
4. Air Frying. Place in the air fryer basket and cook for 40 to 45 minutes until the skin is crispy.
5. Chop before serving.

Nutrition: Calories: 785; Fat:80.7g; Protein:14.2g; Fiber:0g

110. BEEF ROLLS

PREPARATION TIME
10 MINUTES

COOK TIME
14

SERVING
4

INGREDIENTS

- 2 pounds beef steak, opened and flattened with a meat tenderizer
- Salt and black pepper to the taste
- 3 ounces red bell pepper, roasted and chopped
- 6 slices provolone cheese
- 3 tablespoons pesto

DIRECTIONS

1. Arrange flattened beef steak on a cutting board, spread pesto all over, add cheese in a single layer, add bell peppers, salt and pepper to the taste.
2. Roll your steak, secure with toothpicks, season again with salt and pepper, place roll in your air fryer's basket and cook at 400 degrees F for 14 minutes, rotating roll halfway.
3. Leave aside to cool down, cut into 2-inch smaller rolls, arrange on a platter and serve them as an appetizer.
4. Enjoy!

Nutrition: Calories 230, Fat 1, Fiber 3, Carbs 12, Protein 10

111. HOMEMADE CORNED BEEF WITH ONIONS

PREPARATION TIME
5 MINUTES

COOK TIME
50

SERVING
4

INGREDIENTS

- Salt and pepper to taste
- 1 cup water
- 1-pound corned beef brisket, cut into chunks
- 1 tablespoon Dijon mustard
- 1 small onion, chopped

DIRECTIONS

1. Preheat the air fryer to 400oF.
2. Place all ingredients in a baking dish that will fit in the air fryer.
3. Cover with foil.
4. Cook for 35 minutes.
5. Remove foil, mix well, turnover beef, and continue cooking for another 15 minutes.

Nutrition: Calories Nutrition: 238; Carbohydrates: 3.1g; Protein: 17.2g; Fat: 17.1g; Sugar: 1.3g; Sodium:1427mg; Fiber: 0.6g

112. DUO CRISP RIBS

PREPARATION TIME
10 MINUTES

COOK TIME
50

SERVING
2

INGREDIENTS

- 1 rack of pork ribs
- Rub
- 1 1/2 cup broth
- 3 tablespoons Liquid Smoke
- 1 cup Barbecue Sauce

DIRECTIONS

1. Rub the rib rack with spice rub generously.
2. Pour the liquid into the Air fryer Duo Crisp.
3. Set an Air Fryer Basket into the Pot and place the rib rack in the basket.
4. Put on the pressure-cooking lid and seal it.
5. Hit the "Pressure Button" and select 30 minutes of Cooking Time, then press "Start."
6. Once the Air fryer Duo beeps, do a quick release and remove its lid.
7. Remove the ribs and rub them with barbecue sauce.
8. Empty the pot and place the Air Fryer Basket in it.
9. Set the ribs in the basket, and Air fry them for 20 minutes.
10. Serve.

Nutrition: Calories 306 Total Fat 6.4g Saturated Fat 2g Cholesterol 32mg Sodium 196mg Total Carbohydrate 46g Dietary Fiber 0.8g Total Sugars 33.1g Protein 14.7g

113. ROAST BEEF

PREPARATION TIME
10 MINUTES

COOK TIME
15

SERVING
4

INGREDIENTS

- 2 lb. beef roast top
- oil for spraying
- Rub
- salt and pepper to taste
- 2 teaspoon garlic powder
- 1 teaspoon summer savory

DIRECTIONS

1. Whisk all the rub Ingredients: in a small bowl.
2. Liberally rub this mixture over the roast.
3. Place an Air Fryer Basket in the Air fryer Duo and layer it with cooking oil.
4. Set the seasoned roast in the Air Fryer Basket.
5. Put on the Air Fryer lid and seal it.
6. Hit the "Air fry Button" and select 20 minutes of Cooking Time, then press "Start."
7. Once the Air fryer Duo beeps, remove its lid.
8. Turn the roast and continue Air fryer for another 15 minutes.
9. Serve warm.

Nutrition: Calories 427 Total Fat 14.2g Saturated Fat 5.3g Cholesterol 203mg Sodium 1894mg Total Carbohydrate 1.4g Dietary Fiber 0.3g Total Sugars 0.3g Protein 69.1g

114. BASIC PORK CHOPS

PREPARATION TIME
10 MINUTES

COOK TIME
15

SERVING
4

INGREDIENTS

- 4 pork chops, bone-in
- 1 tablespoon olive oil
- 1 teaspoon kosher salt
- 1/2 teaspoon black pepper

DIRECTIONS

1. Liberally season the pork chops with olive oil, salt, and black pepper.
2. Place the pork chops in the basket and spray them with cooking spray.
3. Set the Air Fryer Basket in the Air fryer Duo.
4. Put on the Air Fryer lid and seal it.
5. Hit the "Air fry Button" and select 15 minutes of Cooking Time, then press "Start."
6. Once the Air fryer Duo beeps, remove its lid.
7. Serve and enjoy.

Nutrition: Calories 287 Total Fat 23.4g Saturated Fat 8g Cholesterol 69mg Sodium 637mg Total Carbohydrate 0.2g Dietary Fiber 0.1g Total Sugars 0g Protein 18g

115. BREADED PORK CHOPS

PREPARATION TIME 10 MINUTES

COOK TIME 18

SERVING 4

INGREDIENTS

- 4 boneless, center-cut pork chops, 1-inch thick
- 1 teaspoon Cajun seasoning
- 1 1/2 cups garlic-flavored croutons
- 2 eggs
- cooking spray

DIRECTIONS

1. Grind croutons in a food processor until it forms crumbs.
2. Season the pork chops with Cajun seasoning liberally.
3. Beat eggs in a shallow tray then dip the pork chops in the egg.
4. Coat the dipped chops in the crouton crumbs.
5. Place the breaded pork chops in the basket of the air fryer.
6. Set the Air Fryer Basket and spray the chops with cooking oil.
7. Put on the Air Fryer lid and seal it.
8. Hit the "Air fry Button" and select 18 minutes of Cooking Time, then press "Start."
9. Once the Air fryer Duo beeps, remove its lid.
10. Serve.

Nutrition: Calories 301 Total Fat 12.4g Saturated Fat 2.6g Cholesterol 160mg Sodium 256mg Total Carbohydrate 12.2g Dietary Fiber 0g Total Sugars 0.2g Protein 32.2g

116. BEEF AND BALSAMIC MARINADE

PREPARATION TIME
5 MINUTES

COOK TIME
40

SERVING
4

INGREDIENTS

- 4 medium beef steaks
- 3 garlic cloves; minced
- 1 cup balsamic vinegar
- 2 tbsp. olive oil
- Salt and black pepper to taste.

DIRECTIONS

1. Take a bowl and mix steaks with the rest of the ingredients and toss.
2. Transfer the steaks to your air fryer's basket and cook at 390°F for 35 minutes, flipping them halfway
3. Divide among plates and serve with a side salad.

Nutrition: Calories: 273; Fat: 14g; Fiber: 4g; Carbs: 6g; Protein: 19g

117. CRISPY BRATS

PREPARATION TIME 5 MINUTES
COOK TIME 15
SERVING 4

INGREDIENTS

- 4 (3-oz. beef bratwursts

DIRECTIONS

1. Place brats into the air fryer basket.
2. Adjust the temperature to 375 Degrees F and set the timer for 15 minutes.

Nutrition: Calories: 286; Protein: 18g; Fiber: 0g; Fat: 28g; Carbs: 0g

118. BASIL PORK CHOPS

PREPARATION TIME
5 MINUTES

COOK TIME
30

SERVING
4

INGREDIENTS

- 4 pork chops
- 2 tsp. basil; dried
- ½ tsp. chili powder
- 2 tbsp. olive oil
- A pinch of salt and black pepper

DIRECTIONS

1. In a pan that fits your air fryer, mix all the ingredients, toss.
2. Introduce in the fryer and cook at 400°F for 25 minutes. Divide everything between plates and serve

Nutrition: Calories: 274; Fat: 13g; Fiber: 4g; Carbs: 6g; Protein: 18g

119. BEEF AND RADISHES

PREPARATION TIME 5 MINUTES

COOK TIME 5

SERVING 2

INGREDIENTS

- 1 lb. radishes, quartered
- 2 cups corned beef, cooked and shredded
- 2 spring onions; chopped
- 2 garlic cloves; minced
- A pinch of salt and black pepper

DIRECTIONS

1. In a pan that fits your air fryer, mix the beef with the rest of the ingredients, toss.
2. Put the pan in the fryer and cook at 390°F for 15 minutes
3. Divide everything into bowls and serve.

Nutrition: Calories: 267; Fat: 13g; Fiber: 2g; Carbs: 5g; Protein: 15g

120. HERBED PORK CHOPS

PREPARATION TIME
5 MINUTES

COOK TIME
25

SERVING
4

INGREDIENTS

- 4 pork chops
- 2 tsp. basil; dried
- ½ tsp. chili powder
- 2 tbsp. olive oil
- A pinch of salt and black pepper

DIRECTIONS

1. In a pan that fits your air fryer, mix all the ingredients, toss.
2. Introduce in the fryer and cook at 400°F for 25 minutes. Divide everything between plates and serve

Nutrition: Calories: 274; Fat: 13g; Fiber: 4g; Carbs: 6g; Protein: 18g

121. BEEF TENDERLOIN

PREPARATION TIME
5 MINUTES

COOK TIME
30

SERVING
6

INGREDIENTS

- 1 (2-poundbeef tenderloin, trimmed of visible fat
- 2 tbsp. salted butter; melted.
- 2 tsp. minced roasted garlic
- 3 tbsp. ground 4-peppercorn blend

DIRECTIONS

1. In a small bowl, mix the butter and roasted garlic. Brush it over the beef tenderloin.
2. Place the ground peppercorns onto a plate and roll the tenderloin through them, creating a crust. Place tenderloin into the air fryer basket
3. Adjust the temperature to 400 Degrees F and set the timer for 25 minutes. Flip the tenderloin halfway through cooking. Set aside for 10 minutes before slicing.

Nutrition: Calories: 289; Protein: 37g; Fiber: 9g; Fat: 18g; Carbs: 5g

122. HONEY MUSTARD PORK TENDERLOIN

PREPARATION TIME
15 MINUTES

COOK TIME
25

SERVING
3

INGREDIENTS

- 1-pound pork tenderloin
- 1 tablespoon garlic, minced
- 2 tablespoons soy sauce
- 2 tablespoons honey
- 1 tablespoon Dijon mustard
- 1 tablespoon grain mustard
- 1 teaspoon Sriracha sauce

DIRECTIONS

1. In a large bowl, add all the ingredients except pork and mix well.
2. Add the pork tenderloin and coat with the mixture generously.
3. Refrigerate to marinate for 2-3 hours.
4. Remove the pork tenderloin from bowl, reserving the marinade.
5. Place the pork tenderloin onto the lightly greased cooking tray.
6. Arrange the drip pan in the bottom of Instant Vortex Plus Air Fryer Oven cooking chamber.
7. Select "Air Fry" and then adjust the temperature to 380 degrees F.
8. Set the timer for 25 minutes and press the "Start".
9. When the display shows "Add Food" insert the cooking tray in the center position.
10. When the display shows "Turn Food" turn the pork and oat with the reserved marinade.
11. When cooking time is complete, remove the tray from Vortex and place the pork tenderloin onto a platter for about 10 minutes before slicing.
12. With a sharp knife, cut the pork tenderloin into desired sized slices and serve.

Nutrition: Calories 277 Total Fat 5.7 g Saturated Fat 1.8 g Cholesterol 110 mg Sodium 782 mg Total Carbs 14.2 g Fiber 0.4 g Sugar 11.8 g Protein 40.7 g

6. FISH AND SEAFOOD

123. BUTTER TROUT

PREPARATION TIME 5 MINUTES **COOK TIME** 20 **SERVING** 4

INGREDIENTS

- trout fillets; boneless
- Juice of 1 lime
- 1 tbsp. parsley; chopped.
- tbsp. butter; melted
- Salt and black pepper to taste.

DIRECTIONS

1. Mix the fish fillets with the melted butter, salt and pepper, rub gently, put the fish in your air fryer's basket and cook at 390°F for 6 minutes on each side.
2. Divide between plates and serve with lime juice drizzled on top and with parsley sprinkled at the end.

Nutrition: Calories: 221; Fat: 11g; Fiber: 4g; Carbs: 6g; Protein: 9g

124. PESTO ALMOND SALMON

PREPARATION TIME
5 MINUTES

COOK TIME
15

SERVING
4

INGREDIENTS

- 2: 1 ½-inch-thicksalmon fillets: about 4 oz. each
- ¼ cup sliced almonds, roughly chopped
- ¼ cup pesto
- tbsp. unsalted butter; melted.

DIRECTIONS

1. In a small bowl, mix pesto and almonds. Set aside. Place fillets into a 6-inch round baking dish
2. Brush each fillet with butter and place half of the pesto mixture on the top of each fillet. Place dish into the air fryer basket. Change the temperature to 390 ° F and set the timer for 12 minutes
3. Salmon will easily flake when fully cooked and reach an internal temperature of at least 145 Degrees F. Serve warm.

Nutrition: Calories: 433; Protein: 23.3g; Fiber: 2.4g; Fat: 34.0g; Carbs: 6.1g

125. GARLIC LEMON SHRIMP

PREPARATION TIME
5 MINUTES

COOK TIME
10

SERVING
4

INGREDIENTS

- 8 oz. medium shelled and deveined shrimp
- 1 medium lemon.
- 2 tbsp. unsalted butter; melted.
- ½ tsp. minced garlic
- ½ tsp. Old Bay seasoning

DIRECTIONS

1. Zest lemon and then cut in half. Place shrimp in a large bowl and squeeze juice from ½ lemon on top of them.
2. Add lemon zest to bowl along with remaining ingredients. Toss shrimp until fully coated
3. Pour bowl contents into 6-inch round baking dish. Place into the air fryer basket.
4. Adjust the temperature to 400 Degrees F and set the timer for 6 minutes. Shrimp will be bright pink when fully cooked. Serve warm with pan sauce.

Nutrition: Calories: 190; Protein: 16.4g; Fiber: 0.4g; Fat: 11.8g; Carbs: 2.9g

126. AIR-FRIED CRAB STICKS

PREPARATION TIME
5 MINUTES

COOK TIME
10

SERVING
4

INGREDIENTS

- Crab sticks: 1 package
- Cooking oil spray: as needed

DIRECTIONS

1. Take each of the sticks out of the package and unroll until flat. Tear the sheets into thirds.
2. Arrange them on a plate and lightly spritz using cooking spray. Set the timer for 10 minutes.
3. Note: If you shred the crab meat; you can cut the time in half, but they will also easily fall through the holes in the basket.

Nutrition: Calories: 220 Carbs: 11 g Fat: 13 g Protein: 23 g

127. AIR FRY CAJUN SALMON

PREPARATION TIME
5 MINUTES

COOK TIME
10

SERVING
4

INGREDIENTS

- Salmon fillet; ¾-inch thick: 1)
- Juice of ¼ lemon
- For Breading: Cajun seasoning for coating
- Optional: Sprinkle of sugar

DIRECTIONS

1. Warm the Air Fryer to 356° Fahrenheit: approx. 5 min.).
2. Rinse and pat the salmon dry. Thoroughly coat the fish with the coating mix.
3. Arrange the fillet in the fryer basket and set the timer for seven minutes with the skin side facing upward.
4. Serve with a drizzle of lemon.

Nutrition: Calories: 370 Carbs: 12 g Fat: 10 g Protein: 28 g

128. E-Z CATFISH

PREPARATION TIME
5 MINUTES

COOK TIME
25

SERVING
3

INGREDIENTS

- Olive oil: 1 tbsp.
- Seasoned fish fry: .25 cup
- Catfish fillets: 4

DIRECTIONS

1. Prepare the fryer to 400° Fahrenheit.
2. First, wash the fish, and dry with a paper towel.
3. Dump the seasoning into a large zip-type baggie. Add the fish and shake to cover each fillet. Spray with a spritz of cooking oil spray. Add to the basket.
4. Set the timer for ten minutes. Flip, and reset the timer for ten more minutes. Flip once more and cook for two to three minutes.
5. Once it reaches the desired crispiness, transfer to a plate to serve.

Nutrition: Calories: 290 Carbs: 14 g Fat: 16 g Protein: 30 g

129. FISH NUGGETS

PREPARATION TIME
5 MINUTES

COOK TIME
20

SERVING
4

INGREDIENTS

- Cod fillet: 1 lb.
- Eggs: 3
- Olive oil: 4 tbsp.
- Almond flour: 1 cup
- Gluten-free breadcrumbs: 1 cup

DIRECTIONS

1. Fix the temperature of the Air Fryer at 390° Fahrenheit.
2. Cut the cod into nuggets.
3. Prepare three dishes. Beat the eggs in one. Combine the oil and breadcrumbs in another. The last one will be almond flour.
4. Cover each of the nuggets using the flour, a dip in the eggs, and the breadcrumbs.
5. Arrange the prepared nuggets in the basket and set the timer for 20 minutes. Serve.

Nutrition: Calories: 220 Carbs: 10 g Fat: 12 g Protein: 23 g

130. GRILLED SHRIMP

PREPARATION TIME
5 MINUTES

COOK TIME
10

SERVING
4

INGREDIENTS

- Medium shrimp/prawns: 8
- Melted butter: 1 tbsp.
- Rosemary: 1 sprig
- Pepper and salt: as desired
- Minced garlic cloves: 3

DIRECTIONS

1. Combine all of the fixings in a mixing bowl. Toss well and arrange in the fryer basket.
2. Set the timer for 7 minutes: 356° Fahrenheit and serve.

Nutrition: Calories: 180 Carbs: 2 g Fat: 10 g Protein: 15 g

131. HONEY & SRIRACHA TOSSED CALAMARI

PREPARATION TIME 10 MINUTES

COOK TIME 20

SERVING 2

INGREDIENTS

- Calamari tubes - tentacles if you prefer: .5 lb.
- Club soda: 1 cup
- Flour: 1 cup
- Salt - red pepper & black pepper: 2 dashes each
- Honey: .5 cup+ 1-2 tbsp. Sriracha

DIRECTIONS

1. Fully rinse the calamari and blot it dry using a bunch of paper towels. Slice into rings: .25-inch wide). Toss the rings into a bowl. Pour in the club soda and stir until all are submerged. Wait for about 10 minutes.
2. Sift the salt, flour, red & black pepper. Set aside for now.
3. Dredge the calamari into the flour mixture and set on a platter until ready to fry.
4. Spritz the basket of the Air Fryer with a small amount of cooking oil spray. Arrange the calamari in the basket, careful not to crowd it too much.
5. Set the temperature at 375° Fahrenheit and the timer for 11 minutes.
6. Shake the basket twice during the cooking process, loosening any rings that may stick.
7. Remove from the basket, toss with the sauce, and return to the fryer for two more minutes.
8. Serve with additional sauce as desired.
9. Make the sauce by combining honey, and sriracha, in a small bowl, mix until fully combined.

Nutrition: Calories: 210 Carbs: 5 g Fat: 12 g Protein: 19 g

132. SALMON CROQUETTES

PREPARATION TIME
5 MINUTES

COOK TIME
10

SERVING
4

INGREDIENTS

- Red salmon: 1 lb. can
- Breadcrumbs: 1 cup
- Vegetable oil: .33 cup
- Chopped parsley: half of 1 bunch
- Eggs: 2

DIRECTIONS

1. Set the Air Fryer at 392° Fahrenheit.
2. Drain and mash the salmon. Whisk and add the eggs and parsley.
3. In another dish, mix the breadcrumbs and oil.
4. Prepare 16 croquettes using the breadcrumb mixture.
5. Arrange in the preheated fryer basket for seven minutes.
6. Serve.

Nutrition: Calories: 240 Carbs: 7 g Fat: 16 g Protein: 30 g

133. SPICY COD

PREPARATION TIME
5 MINUTES

COOK TIME
10

SERVING
4

INGREDIENTS

- 4 cod fillets; boneless
- 2 tbsp. assorted chili peppers
- 1 lemon; sliced
- Juice of 1 lemon
- Salt and black pepper to taste

DIRECTIONS

1. In your air fryer, mix the cod with the chili pepper, lemon juice, salt and pepper
2. Arrange the lemon slices on top and cook at 360°F for 10 minutes. Divide the fillets between plates and serve.

Nutrition: Calories: 250 Carbs: 13 g Fat: 13 g Protein: 29 g

134. AIR FRIED LOBSTER TAILS

PREPARATION TIME
5 MINUTES

COOK TIME
10

SERVING
2

INGREDIENTS

- 2 tablespoons unsalted butter, melted
- 1 tablespoon minced garlic
- 1 teaspoon salt
- 1 tablespoon minced fresh chives
- 2 (4- to 6-ounce) frozen lobster tails

DIRECTIONS

1. Preparing the Ingredients
2. In a bowl, put the butter, garlic, salt, and chives then mix.
3. Butterfly the lobster tail: Starting at the meaty end of the tail, use kitchen shears to cut down the center of the top shell. Stop when you reach the fanned, wide part of the tail. Carefully spread apart the meat and the shell along the cut line, but keep the meat attached where it connects to the wide part of the tail. Use your hand to disconnect the meat from the bottom of the shell gently. Lift the meat up and out of the shell (keeping it attached at the wide end). Close the shell under the meat, so the meat rests on top of the shell.
4. Place the lobster in the air fryer basket and generously brush the butter mixture over the meat.
5. Air Frying. Set the temperature of your AF to 380°F. Set the timer and steam for 4 minutes.
6. Open the air fryer and rotate the lobster tails. Brush them with more of the butter mixture. Reset the timer and steam for 4 minutes more. The lobster is done when the meat is opaque.

Nutrition: Calories: 255; Fat: 13g; Carbohydrate: 2g; Protein: 32g; Sodium: 1453mg

135. AIR FRYER SALMON

PREPARATION TIME
5 MINUTES

COOK TIME
10

SERVING
2

INGREDIENTS

- ½ tsp. salt
- ½ tsp. garlic powder
- ½ tsp. smoked paprika
- Salmon

DIRECTIONS

1. Preparing the Ingredients. Mix spices together and sprinkle onto salmon. Place seasoned salmon into the Air fryer.
2. Air Frying. Close crisping lid. Set temperature to 400°F, and set time to 10 minutes.

Nutrition: Calories: 185; Fat: 11g; Protein:21g; Sugar:0g

136. SIMPLE SCALLOPS

PREPARATION TIME
5 MINUTES

COOK TIME
5

SERVING
4

INGREDIENTS

- 12 medium sea scallops
- 1 teaspoon fine sea salt
- ground black pepper as desired
- Fresh thyme leaves, for garnish (optional)

DIRECTIONS

1. Preparing the Ingredients. Grease the air fryer basket with avocado oil. Preheat the air fryer to 390°F. Rinse the scallops and pat completely dry. Spray avocado oil on the scallops and season them with the salt and pepper.
2. Air Frying. Place them in the air fryer basket, spacing them apart (if you're using a smaller air fryer, work in batches if necessary). Flip the scallops after cooking for 2 minutes, and cook for another 2 minutes, or until cooked through and no longer translucent. Garnish with ground black pepper and thyme leaves, if desired. Best served fresh.

Nutrition: Calories: 170 Carbs: 8 g Fat: 11 g Protein: 17 g

137. 3-INGREDIENT AIR FRYER CATFISH

PREPARATION TIME
5 MINUTES

COOK TIME
15

SERVING
4

INGREDIENTS

- 1 tbsp. chopped parsley
- 1 tbsp. olive oil
- ¼ C. seasoned fish fry
- 4 catfish fillets

DIRECTIONS

1. Preparing the Ingredients. Ensure your air fryer is preheated to 400 degrees.
2. Rinse off catfish fillets and pat dry. Add fish fry seasoning to Ziploc baggie, then catfish. Shake bag and ensure fish gets well coated. Spray each fillet with olive oil. Add fillets to air fryer basket.
3. Air Frying. Set temperature to 400°F, and set time to 10 minutes. Cook 10 minutes. Then flip and cook another 2-3 minutes.

Nutrition: Calories: 208; Fat: 5g; Protein:17g; Sugar:0.5g

138. PECAN-CRUSTED CATFISH

PREPARATION TIME
5 MINUTES

COOK TIME
12

SERVING
4

INGREDIENTS

- ½ cup pecan meal
- 1 teaspoon fine sea salt
- ¼ teaspoon ground black pepper
- 4 (4-ounce) catfish fillets

FOR GARNISH (OPTIONAL):
- Fresh oregano

DIRECTIONS

1. Preparing the Ingredients. Grease the air fryer basket with avocado oil. Preheat the air fryer to 375°F. In a large bowl, mix the pecan meal, salt, and pepper. One at a time, dredge the catfish fillets in the mixture, coating them well. Use your hands to press the pecan meal into the fillets. Spray the fish with avocado oil and place them in the air fryer basket.
2. Air Frying. Cook the coated catfish for 12 minutes, or until it flakes easily and is no longer translucent in the center, flipping halfway through. Garnish with oregano sprigs and pecan halves, if desired.

Nutrition: Calories 162; Fat 11g; Protein 17g; Total carbs 1g; Fiber 1g

139. FLYING FISH

PREPARATION TIME
5 MINUTES

COOK TIME
12

SERVING
4

INGREDIENTS

- Tbsp Oil
- 3–4 oz Breadcrumbs
- 1 Whisked Whole Egg in a Saucer/Soup Plate
- 4 Fresh Fish Fillets
- Fresh Lemon (For serving)

DIRECTIONS

1. Preparing the Ingredients. Warm up the air fryer to 350° F. Mix the crumbs and oil until it looks nice and loose. Dip the fish in the egg and coat lightly, then move on to the crumbs. Make sure the fillet is covered evenly.
2. Air Frying. Cook in the air fryer basket for roughly 12 minutes; depending on the size of the fillets you are using. Serve with fresh lemon & chips to complete the duo.

Nutrition: Calories: 180 Carbs: 9 g Fat: 12 g Protein: 19 g

140. AIR FRYER FISH TACOS

PREPARATION TIME
5 MINUTES

COOK TIME
15

SERVING
4

INGREDIENTS

- 1 pound cod
- 1 tbsp. cumin
- ½ tbsp. chili powder
- 1 ½ C. coconut flour
- 10 ounces Mexican beer
- 2 eggs

DIRECTIONS

1. Preparing the Ingredients. Whisk beer and eggs together. Whisk flour, pepper, salt, cumin, and chili powder together. Slice cod into large pieces and coat in egg mixture then flour mixture.
2. Air Frying. Spray bottom of your air fryer basket with olive oil and add coated cod pieces. Cook 15 minutes at 375 degrees.
3. Serve on lettuce leaves topped with homemade salsa.

Nutrition: Calories: 178; Carbs:61g; Fat:10g; Protein:19g; Sugar:1g

141. BACON WRAPPED SCALLOPS

PREPARATION TIME
5 MINUTES

COOK TIME
15

SERVING
4

INGREDIENTS

- 1 tsp. paprika
- 1 tsp. lemon pepper
- 5 slices of center-cut bacon
- 20 raw sea scallops

DIRECTIONS

1. Preparing the Ingredients. Rinse and drain scallops, placing on paper towels to soak up excess moisture. Cut slices of bacon into 4 pieces. With a piece of bacon, wrap each scallop, then using toothpicks to secure. Sprinkle wrapped scallops with paprika and lemon pepper.
2. Air Frying. Spray air fryer basket with olive oil and add scallops.
3. Cook 5-6 minutes at 400 degrees, making sure to flip halfway through

Nutrition: Calories: 389; Carbs:63g; Fat:17g; Protein:21g; Sugar:1g

142. QUICK FRIED CATFISH

PREPARATION TIME
5 MINUTES

COOK TIME
15

SERVING
4

INGREDIENTS

- 3/4 cups Original Bisquick™ mix
- 1/2 cup yellow cornmeal
- 1 tablespoon seafood seasoning
- 4 catfish fillets (4-6 oz. each)
- 1/2 cup ranch dressing

DIRECTIONS

1. Preparing the Ingredients.
2. In a bowl mix the Bisquick mix, cornmeal, and seafood seasoning together. Pat the filets dry, then brush them with ranch dressing. Press the filets into the Bisquick mix on both sides until the filet is evenly coated.
3. Air Frying.
4. Cook in your air fryer at 360 degrees for 15 minutes, flip the filets halfway through. Serve.

Nutrition: Calories: 372; Fat:16g; Protein:28g; Fiber:1.7g

143. AIR-FRIED HERBED SHRIMP

PREPARATION TIME
2 MINUTES

COOK TIME
5

SERVING
4

INGREDIENTS

- One ¼ lb. shrimp, peeled and deveined
- ½ teaspoon paprika
- One tablespoon olive oil
- ¼ cayenne pepper
- ½ teaspoon Old Bay seasoning

DIRECTIONS

1. Preheat air fryer to 400° Fahrenheit. Mix all the ingredients in a bowl. Place the seasoned shrimp into the air fryer basket and cook for 5-minutes.

Nutrition: Calories: 300 Total Fat: 9.3g Carbs: 8.2g Protein: 14.6g

144. BREADED FLOUNDER

PREPARATION TIME
15 MINUTES

COOK TIME
12

SERVING
3

INGREDIENTS

- 1 egg
- 1 cup dry breadcrumbs
- ¼ cup vegetable oil
- 3 (6-oz.) flounder fillets
- 1 lemon, sliced

DIRECTIONS

1. In a shallow bowl, beat the egg
2. In another bowl, add the breadcrumbs and oil and mix until crumbly mixture is formed.
3. Dip flounder fillets into the beaten egg and then, coat with the breadcrumb mixture.
4. Press "Power Button" of Air Fry Oven and turn the dial to select the "Air Fry" mode.
5. Press the Time button and again turn the dial to set the Cooking Time to 12 minutes.
6. Now push the Temp button and rotate the dial to set the temperature at 356 degrees F.
7. Press "Start/Pause" button to start.
8. When the unit beeps to show that it is preheated, open the lid.
9. Arrange the flounder fillets in greased "Air Fry Basket" and insert in the oven.
10. Plate with lemon slices and serve hot.

Nutrition: Calories 524 Total Fat 24.2 g Saturated Fat 5.1 g Cholesterol 170 mg Sodium 463 mg Total Carbs 26.5 g Fiber 1.5 g Sugar 2.5 g Protein 47.8g

145. SIMPLE HADDOCK

PREPARATION TIME
15 MINUTES

COOK TIME
8

SERVING
2

INGREDIENTS

- 2 (6-oz.) haddock fillets
- 1 tablespoon olive oil
- Salt and ground black pepper, as required

DIRECTIONS

1. Coat the fish fillets with oil and then, sprinkle with salt and black pepper.
2. Press "Power Button" of Air Fry Oven and turn the dial to select the "Air Fry" mode.
3. Press the Time button and again turn the dial to set the Cooking Time to 8 minutes.
4. Now push the Temp button and rotate the dial to set the temperature at 355 degrees F.
5. Press "Start/Pause" button to start.
6. When the unit beeps to show that it is preheated, open the lid.
7. Arrange the haddock fillets in greased "Air Fry Basket" and insert in the oven.
8. Serve hot.

Nutrition: Calories 251 Total Fat 8.6 g Saturated Fat 1.3 g Cholesterol 126 mg Sodium 226 mg Total Carbs 0 g Fiber 0 g Sugar 0 g Protein 41.2 g

146. BREADED HAKE

PREPARATION TIME
15 MINUTES

COOK TIME
12

SERVING
4

INGREDIENTS

- 1 egg
- 4 oz. breadcrumbs
- 2 tablespoons vegetable oil
- 4 (6-oz.) hake fillets
- 1 lemon, cut into wedges

DIRECTIONS

1. In a shallow bowl, whisk the egg.
2. In another bowl, add the breadcrumbs, and oil and mix until a crumbly mixture forms.
3. Dip fish fillets into the egg and then, coat with the bread crumbs mixture.
4. Press "Power Button" of Air Fry Oven and turn the dial to select the "Air Fry" mode.
5. Press the Time button and again turn the dial to set the Cooking Time to 12 minutes.
6. Now push the Temp button and rotate the dial to set the temperature at 350 degrees F.
7. Press "Start/Pause" button to start.
8. When the unit beeps to show that it is preheated, open the lid.
9. Arrange the hake fillets in greased "Air Fry Basket" and insert in the oven.
10. Serve hot.

Nutrition: Calories 297 Total Fat 10.6 g Saturated Fat 2 g Cholesterol 89 mg Sodium 439 mg Total Carbs 22 g Fiber 1.4 g Sugar 1.9 g Protein 29.2 g

147. SESAME SEEDS COATED TUNA

PREPARATION TIME
15 MINUTES

COOK TIME
6

SERVING
2

INGREDIENTS

- 1 egg white
- ¼ cup white sesame seeds
- 1 tablespoon black sesame seeds
- Salt and ground black pepper, as required
- 2 (6-oz.) tuna steaks

DIRECTIONS

1. In a bowl, beat the egg white.
2. In another bowl, mix together the sesame seeds, salt, and black pepper.
3. Dip the tuna steaks into egg white and then, coat with the sesame seeds mixture.
4. Press "Power Button" of Air Fry Oven and turn the dial to select the "Air Fry" mode.
5. Press the Time button and again turn the dial to set the Cooking Time to 6 minutes.
6. Now push the Temp button and rotate the dial to set the temperature at 400 degrees F.
7. Press "Start/Pause" button to start.
8. When the unit beeps to show that it is preheated, open the lid.
9. Arrange the tuna steaks in greased "Air Fry Basket" and insert in the oven.
10. Flip the tuna steaks once halfway through.
11. Serve hot.

Nutrition: Calories 450 Total Fat 21.9 g Saturated Fat 4.3 g Cholesterol 83 mg Sodium 182 mg Total Carbs 5.4 g Fiber 2.7 g Sugar 0.2 g Protein 56.7 g

148. CHEESE AND HAM PATTIES

PREPARATION TIME
10 MINUTES

COOK TIME
10

SERVING
4

INGREDIENTS

- 1 puff pastry sheet
- 4 handfuls mozzarella cheese, grated
- 4 teaspoons mustard
- 8 ham slices, chopped

DIRECTIONS

1. Spread out puff pastry on a clean surface and cut it in 12 squares.
2. Divide cheese, ham, and mustard on half of them, top with the other halves, and seal the edges.
3. Place all the patties in your air fryer's basket and cook at 370 degrees F for 10 minutes.
4. Divide the patties between plates and serve.

Nutrition: Calories 212, Fat 12, Fiber 7, Carbs 14, Protein 8

149. AIR-FRIED SEAFOOD

PREPARATION TIME
10 MINUTES

COOK TIME
10

SERVING
4

INGREDIENTS

- 1 lb. fresh scallops, mussels, fish fillets, prawns, shrimp
- 2 eggs, lightly beaten
- Salt and black pepper
- 1 cup breadcrumbs mixed with the zest of 1 lemon
- Cooking spray

DIRECTIONS

1. Clean the seafood as needed.
2. Dip each piece into the egg; and season with salt and pepper.
3. Coat in the crumbs and spray with oil.
4. Arrange into the air fryer and cook for 6 minutes at 4000 F. turning once halfway through.
5. Serve and Enjoy!

Nutrition: Calories: 133 Protein: 17.4 grams Fat: 3.1 grams Carbohydrates: 8.2 grams

150. FISH WITH CHIPS

PREPARATION TIME
5 MINUTES

COOK TIME
20

SERVING
2

INGREDIENTS

- 1 cod fillet (6 ounces)
- 3 cups salt
- 3 cups vinegar-flavored kettle cooked chips
- ¼ cup buttermilk
- salt and pepper to taste

DIRECTIONS

1. Mix to combine the buttermilk, pepper, and salt in a bowl. Put the cod and leave to soak for 5 minutes
2. Put the chips in a food processor and process until crushed. Transfer to a shallow bowl. Coat the fillet with the crushed chips.
3. Put the coated fillet in the air frying basket. Cook for 12 minutes at 4000 F.
4. Serve and Enjoy!

Nutrition: Calories: 646 Protein: 41 grams Fat: 33 grams Carbohydrates: 48 grams

151. CRUMBLY FISHCAKES

PREPARATION TIME
5 MINUTES

COOK TIME
10

SERVING
4

INGREDIENTS

- 8 oz. salmon, cooked
- 1 ½ oz. potatoes, mashed
- A handful of parsley, chopped
- Zest of 1 lemon
- 1 ¾ oz. plain flour

DIRECTIONS

1. Carefully flakes the salmon. In a bowl, mix flaked salmon, zest, capers, dill, and mashed potatoes.
2. From small cakes using the mixture and dust the cakes with flour; refrigerate for 60 minutes.
3. Preheat your air fryer to 3500 F. and cook the cakes for 7 minutes. Serve chilled.

Nutrition: Calories: 210 Protein: 10 grams Fat: 7 grams Carbohydrates: 25 grams

152. BACON WRAPPED SHRIMP

PREPARATION TIME
10 MINUTES

COOK TIME
20

SERVING
4

INGREDIENTS

- 16 thin slices of bacon
- 16 pieces of tiger shrimp (peeled and deveined)

DIRECTIONS

1. With a slice of bacon, wrap each shrimp. Put all the finished pieces in tray and chill for 20 minutes.
2. Arrange the bacon-wrapped shrimp in the air frying basket. Cook for 7 minutes at 3900 F. Transfer to a plate lined with paper towels to drain before serving.

Nutrition: Calories: 436 Protein: 32 grams Fat: 41.01 grams Carbohydrates: 0.8 grams

153. CRAB LEGS

PREPARATION TIME 10 MINUTES

COOK TIME 10

SERVING 4

INGREDIENTS

- 3 lb. crab legs
- ¼ cup salted butter, melted and divided
- ½ lemon, juiced
- ¼ tsp. garlic powder

DIRECTIONS

1. In a bowl, toss the crab legs and two tablespoons of the melted butter together. Place the crab legs in the basket of the fryer.
2. Cook at 400°F for fifteen minutes, giving the basket a good shake halfway through.
3. Combine the remaining butter with the lemon juice and garlic powder.
4. Crack open the cooked crab legs and remove the meat. Serve with the butter dip on the side, and enjoy!

Nutrition: Calories 272, Fat 19, Fiber 9, Carbs 18, Protein 12

154. FISH STICKS

PREPARATION TIME
5 MINUTES

COOK TIME
10

SERVING
4

INGREDIENTS

- 1 lb. whitefish
- 2 tbsp. Dijon mustard
- ¼ cup mayonnaise
- 1 ½ cup pork rinds, finely ground
- ¾ tsp. Cajun seasoning

DIRECTIONS

1. Place the fish on a tissue to dry it off, then cut it up into slices about two inches thick.
2. In one bowl, combine the mustard and mayonnaise, and in another, the Cajun seasoning and pork rinds.
3. Coat the fish firstly in the mayo-mustard mixture, then in the Cajun-pork rind mixture. Give each slice a shake to remove any surplus. Then place the fish sticks in the basket of the air flyer.
4. Cook at 400°F for five minutes. Turn the fish sticks over and cook for another five minutes on the other side.
5. Serve warm with a dipping sauce of your choosing and enjoy.

Nutrition: Calories 212, Fat 12, Fiber 7, Carbs 14, Protein 8

155. CRUSTY PESTO SALMON

PREPARATION TIME
5 MINUTES

COOK TIME
10

SERVING
2

INGREDIENTS

- ¼ cup almonds, roughly chopped
- ¼ cup pesto
- 2 x 4-oz. salmon fillets
- 2 tbsp. unsalted butter, melted

DIRECTIONS

1. Mix the almonds and pesto together.
2. Place the salmon fillets in a round baking dish, roughly six inches in diameter.
3. Brush the fillets with butter, followed by the pesto mixture, ensuring to coat both the top and bottom. Put the baking dish inside the fryer.
4. Cook for twelve minutes at 390°F.
5. The salmon is ready when it flakes easily when prodded with a fork. Serve warm.

Nutrition: Calories 354 Fat 21 Carbs 23 Protein 19

156. SALMON PATTIES

PREPARATION TIME
5 MINUTES

COOK TIME
10

SERVING
4

INGREDIENTS

- 1 tsp. chili powder
- 2 tbsp. full-fat mayonnaise
- ¼ cup ground pork rinds
- 2 x 5-oz. pouches of cooked pink salmon
- 1 egg

DIRECTIONS

1. Stir everything together to prepare the patty mixture. If the mixture is dry or falling apart, add in more pork rinds as necessary.
2. Take equal-sized amounts of the mixture to form four patties, before placing the patties in the basket of your air fryer.
3. Cook at 400°F for eight minutes.
4. Halfway through cooking, flip the patties over. Once they are crispy, serve with the toppings of your choice and enjoy.

Nutrition: Calories 325 Fat 21 Carbs 18 Protein 29

157. CAJUN SALMON

PREPARATION TIME
5 MINUTES

COOK TIME
10

SERVING
4

INGREDIENTS

- 2 4-oz skinless salmon fillets
- 2 tbsp. unsalted butter, melted
- 1 pinch ground cayenne pepper
- 1 tsp. paprika
- ½ tsp. garlic pepper

DIRECTIONS

1. Using a brush, apply the butter to the salmon fillets.
2. Combine the other ingredients and massage this mixture into the fillets. Lay the fish inside your fryer.
3. Cook for seven minutes at 390°F.
4. When the salmon is ready it should flake apart easily.
5. Enjoy with the sides of your choosing.

Nutrition: Calories 383 Fat 12 Carbs 29 Protein 31

158. BUTTERY COD

PREPARATION TIME
5 MINUTES

COOK TIME
10

SERVING
4

INGREDIENTS

- 2 x 4-oz. cod fillets
- 2 tbsp. salted butter, melted
- 1 tsp. Old Bay seasoning
- ½ medium lemon, sliced

DIRECTIONS

1. Place the cod fillets in a dish.
2. Brush with melted butter, season with Old Bay, and top with some lemon slices.
3. Wrap the fish in aluminum foil and put into your fryer.
4. Cook for eight minutes at 350°F.
5. The cod is ready when it flakes easily. Serve hot.

Nutrition: Calories 354 Fat 21 Carbs 23 Protein 19

159. SESAME TUNA STEAK

PREPARATION TIME
5 MINUTES

COOK TIME
10

SERVING
4

INGREDIENTS

- 1 tbsp. coconut oil, melted
- 2 x 6-oz. tuna steaks
- ½ tsp. garlic powder
- 2 tsp. black sesame seeds
- 2 tsp. white sesame seeds

DIRECTIONS

1. Apply the coconut oil to the tuna steaks with a brunch, then season with garlic powder.
2. Combine the black and white sesame seeds. Embed them in the tuna steaks, covering the fish all over. Place the tuna into your air fryer.
3. Cook for eight minutes at 400°F, turning the fish halfway through.
4. The tuna steaks are ready when they have reached a temperature of 145°F. Serve straightaway.

Nutrition: Calories 343 Fat 11 Carbs 27 Protein 25

160. LEMON GARLIC SHRIMP

PREPARATION TIME
5 MINUTES

COOK TIME
10

SERVING
4

INGREDIENTS

- 1 medium lemon
- ½ lb. medium shrimp, shelled and deveined
- ½ tsp. Old Bay seasoning
- 2 tbsp. unsalted butter, melted
- ½ tsp. minced garlic

DIRECTIONS

1. Grate the lemon rind into a bowl. Cut the lemon in half then juice it over the same bowl. Toss in the shrimp, Old Bay, and butter, mixing everything to make sure the shrimp is completely covered.
2. Transfer to a round baking dish roughly six inches wide, then place this dish in your air fryer.
3. Cook at 400°F for six minutes. The shrimp is ready when it becomes a bright pink color.
4. Serve hot, drizzling any leftover sauce over the shrimp.

Nutrition: Calories 374 Fat 14 Carbs 18 Protein 21

161. FOIL PACKET SALMON

PREPARATION TIME
5 MINUTES

COOK TIME
10

SERVING
4

INGREDIENTS

- 2 x 4-oz. skinless salmon fillets
- 2 tbsp. unsalted butter, melted
- ½ tsp. garlic powder
- 1 medium lemon
- ½ tsp. dried dill

DIRECTIONS

1. Take a sheet of foil and cut into two squares measuring roughly 5" x 5". Lay each of the salmon fillets at the center of each piece. Brush both fillets with a tablespoon of bullet and season with a quarter-teaspoon of garlic powder.
2. Halve the lemon and grate the skin of one half over the fish. Cut four half-slices of lemon, using two to top each fillet. Season each fillet with a quarter-teaspoon of dill.
3. Fold the tops and sides of the aluminum foil over the fish to create a kind of packet. Place each one in the fryer.
4. Cook for twelve minutes at 400°F.
5. The salmon is ready when it flakes easily. Serve hot.

Nutrition: Calories 365 Fat 16 Carbs 18 Protein 23

162. FOIL PACKET LOBSTER TAIL

PREPARATION TIME
5 MINUTES

COOK TIME
10

SERVING
4

INGREDIENTS

- 2 x 6-oz. lobster tail halves
- 2 tbsp. salted butter, melted
- ½ medium lemon, juiced
- ½ tsp. Old Bay seasoning
- 1 tsp. dried parsley

DIRECTIONS

1. Lay each lobster on a sheet of aluminum foil. Pour a light drizzle of melted butter and lemon juice over each one, and season with Old Bay.
2. Fold down the sides and ends of the foil to seal the lobster. Place each one in the fryer.
3. Cook at 375°F for twelve minutes.
4. Just before serving, top the lobster with dried parsley.

Nutrition: Calories 369 Fat 19 Carbs 25 Protein 28

163. AVOCADO SHRIMP

PREPARATION TIME
5 MINUTES

COOK TIME
10

SERVING
4

INGREDIENTS

- ½ cup onion, chopped
- 2 lb. shrimp
- 1 tbsp. seasoned salt
- 1 avocado
- ½ cup pecans, chopped

DIRECTIONS

1. Pre-heat the fryer at 400°F.
2. Put the chopped onion in the basket of the fryer and spritz with some cooking spray. Leave to cook for five minutes.
3. Add the shrimp and set the timer for a further five minutes. Sprinkle with some seasoned salt, then allow to cook for an additional five minutes.
4. During these last five minutes, halve your avocado and remove the pit. Cube each half, then scoop out the flesh.
5. Take care when removing the shrimp from the fryer. Place it on a dish and top with the avocado and the chopped pecans.

Nutrition: Calories 384 Fat 24 Carbs 13 Protein 39

164. CITRUSY BRANZINI ON THE GRILL

PREPARATION TIME
5 MINUTES

COOK TIME
15

SERVING
4

INGREDIENTS

- branzini fillets
- Salt and pepper to taste
- lemons, juice freshly squeezed
- oranges, juice freshly squeezed

DIRECTIONS

1. Place all ingredients in a Ziploc bag. Keep it in the fridge for 2 hours.
2. Preheat the air fryer at 3900F.
3. Place the grill pan attachment in the air fryer.
4. Place the fish on the grill pan and cook for 15 minutes until the fish is flaky.

Nutrition: Calories: 318; Carbs: 20.8g; Protein: 23.5g; Fat: 15.6g

165. CAJUN-SEASONED LEMON SALMON

PREPARATION TIME
5 MINUTES

COOK TIME
10

SERVING
4

INGREDIENTS

- 1 salmon fillet
- 1 teaspoon Cajun seasoning
- lemon wedges, for serving
- 1 teaspoon liquid stevia
- ½ lemon, juiced

DIRECTIONS

1. Preheat your air fryer to 350° Fahrenheit. Combine lemon juice and liquid stevia and coat salmon with this mixture. Sprinkle Cajun seasoning all over salmon. Place salmon on parchment paper in air fryer and cook for 7-minutes. Serve with lemon wedges.

Nutrition: Calories: 287, Total Fat: 9.3g, Carbs: 8.4g, Protein: 15.3g

166. GRILLED SALMON FILLETS

PREPARATION TIME
5 MINUTES

COOK TIME
10

SERVING
4

INGREDIENTS

- salmon fillets
- tablespoons olive oil
- 1/3 cup of light soy sauce
- 1/3 cup of water
- Salt and black pepper to taste

DIRECTIONS

1. Season salmon fillets with salt and pepper. Mix what's left of the ingredients in a bowl. Allow the salmon fillets to marinate in mixture for 2-hours. Preheat your air fryer to 355° Fahrenheit for 5-minutes. Drain salmon fillets and air fry for 8-minutes.

Nutrition: Calories: 302, Total Fat: 8.6g, Carbs: 7.3g, Protein: 15.3g

167. CHEESY BREADED SALMON

PREPARATION TIME
5 MINUTES

COOK TIME
20

SERVING
4

INGREDIENTS

- cups breadcrumbs
- salmon fillets
- eggs, beaten
- 1 cup Swiss cheese, shredded

DIRECTIONS

1. Preheat your air fryer to 390° Fahrenheit. Dip each salmon filet into eggs. Top with Swiss cheese. Dip into breadcrumbs, coating entire fish. Put into an oven-safe dish and cook for 20-minutes.

Nutrition: Calories: 296, Total Fat: 9.2g, Carbs: 8.7g, Protein: 15.2g

168. COCONUT CRUSTED SHRIMP

PREPARATION TIME
15 MINUTES

COOK TIME
40

SERVING
4

INGREDIENTS

- ounces coconut milk
- ½ cup sweetened coconut, shredded
- ½ cup panko breadcrumbs
- 1-pound large shrimp, peeled and deveined
- Salt and black pepper, to taste

DIRECTIONS

1. Preheat the Air fryer to 350 o F and grease an Air fryer basket.
2. Place the coconut milk in a shallow bowl.
3. Mix coconut, breadcrumbs, salt, and black pepper in another bowl.
4. Dip each shrimp into coconut milk and finally, dredge in the coconut mixture.
5. Arrange half of the shrimps into the Air fryer basket and cook for about 20 minutes.
6. Dish out the shrimps onto serving plates and repeat with the remaining mixture to serve.

Nutrition: Calories: 408, Fats: 23.7g, Carbohydrates: 11.7g, Sugar: 3.4g, Proteins: 31g,

169. RICE FLOUR COATED SHRIMP

PREPARATION TIME
20 MINUTES

COOK TIME
20

SERVING
3

INGREDIENTS

- tablespoons rice flour
- 1-pound shrimp, peeled and deveined
- tablespoons olive oil
- 1 teaspoon powdered sugar
- Salt and black pepper, as required

DIRECTIONS

1. Preheat the Air fryer to 325 o F and grease an Air fryer basket.
2. Mix rice flour, olive oil, sugar, salt, and black pepper in a bowl.
3. Stir in the shrimp and transfer half of the shrimp to the Air fryer basket.
4. Cook for about 10 minutes, flipping once in between.
5. Dish out the mixture onto serving plates and repeat with the remaining mixture.

Nutrition: Calories: 299, Fat: 12g, Carbohydrates: 11.1g, Sugar: 0.8g, Protein: 35g, Sodium: 419mg

170. BUTTERED SCALLOPS

PREPARATION TIME
15 MINUTES

COOK TIME
4

SERVING
2

INGREDIENTS

- ¾ pound sea scallops, cleaned and patted very dry
- 1 tablespoon butter, melted
- ½ tablespoon fresh thyme, minced
- Salt and black pepper, as required

DIRECTIONS

1. Preheat the Air fryer to 390 o F and grease an Air fryer basket.
2. Mix scallops, butter, thyme, salt, and black pepper in a bowl.
3. Arrange scallops in the Air fryer basket and cook for about 4 minutes.
4. Dish out the scallops in a platter and serve hot.

Nutrition: Calories: 202, Fat: 7.1g, Carbohydrates: 4.4g, Sugar: 0g, Protein: 28.7g,

7. SNACK AND APPETIZER

171. BUTTERNUT SQUASH WITH THYME

PREPARATION TIME
5 MINUTES

COOK TIME
20

SERVING
4

INGREDIENTS

- 2 cups peeled, butternut squash, cubed
- 1 tbsp olive oil
- ¼ tsp salt
- ¼ tsp black pepper
- ¼ tsp dried thyme
- 1 tbsp finely chopped fresh parsley

DIRECTIONS

1. In a bowl, add squash, oil, salt, pepper, and thyme, and toss until squash is well-coated.
2. Place squash in the air fryer and cook for 14 minutes at 360 F.
3. When ready, sprinkle with freshly chopped parsley and serve chilled.

Nutrition: Calories 219 Fat 4.3 g Carbs 9.4 g Protein 7.8 g

172. CHICKEN BREASTS IN GOLDEN CRUMB

PREPARATION TIME
10 MINUTES

COOK TIME
25

SERVING
4

INGREDIENTS

- 1 ½ lb. chicken breasts, boneless, cut into strips
- 1 egg, lightly beaten
- 1 cup seasoned breadcrumbs
- Salt and black pepper to taste
- ½ tsp dried oregano

DIRECTIONS

1. Preheat the air fryer to 390 F. Season the chicken with oregano, salt, and black pepper. In a small bowl, whisk in some salt and pepper to the beaten egg. In a separate bowl, add the crumbs. Dip chicken tenders in the egg wash, then in the crumbs.
2. Roll the strips in the breadcrumbs and press firmly, so the breadcrumbs stick well. Spray the chicken tenders with cooking spray and arrange them in the air fryer. Cook for 14 minutes, until no longer pink in the center, and nice and crispy on the outside.

Nutrition: Calories 223, Fat 3.2 g Carbs 4.3 g Protein 5 g

173. YOGURT CHICKEN TACOS

PREPARATION TIME
5 MINUTES

COOK TIME
20

SERVING
4

INGREDIENTS

- 1 cup cooked chicken, shredded
- 1 cup shredded mozzarella cheese
- ¼ cup salsa
- ¼ cup Greek yogurt
- Salt and ground black pepper
- 8 flour tortillas

DIRECTIONS

1. In a bowl, mix chicken, cheese, salsa, and yogurt, and season with salt and pepper. Spray one side of the tortilla with cooking spray. Lay 2 tbsp of the chicken mixture at the center of the non-oiled side of each tortilla.
2. Roll tightly around the mixture. Arrange taquitos into your air fryer basket, without overcrowding. Cook in batches if needed. Place the seam side down, or it will unravel during cooking crisps.
3. Cook it for 12 to 14 minutes, or until crispy, at 380 F.

Nutrition: Calories 312 Fat 3 g Carbs 6.5 g Protein 6.2 g

174. FLAWLESS KALE CHIPS

PREPARATION TIME
5 MINUTES

COOK TIME
20

SERVING
4

INGREDIENTS

- 4 cups chopped kale leaves; stems removed
- 2 tbsp olive oil
- 1 tsp garlic powder
- ½ tsp salt
- ¼ tsp onion powder
- ¼ tsp black pepper

DIRECTIONS

1. In a bowl, mix kale and oil together, until well-coated. Add in garlic, salt, onion, and pepper and toss until well-coated. Arrange half the kale leaves to air fryer, in a single layer.
2. Cook for 8 minutes at 350 F, shaking once halfway through. Remove chips to a sheet to cool; do not touch.

Nutrition: Calories 312 Fat 5.3 g Carbs 5 g Protein 7 g

175. CHEESE FISH BALLS

PREPARATION TIME
5 MINUTES

COOK TIME
40

SERVING
6

INGREDIENTS

- 1 cup smoked fish, flaked
- 2 cups cooked rice
- 2 eggs, lightly beaten
- 1 cup grated Grana Padano cheese
- ¼ cup finely chopped thyme
- Salt and black pepper to taste
- 1 cup panko crumbs

DIRECTIONS

1. In a bowl, add fish, rice, eggs, Parmesan cheese, thyme, salt and pepper into a bowl; stir to combine. Shape the mixture into 12 even-sized balls. Roll the balls in the crumbs then spray with oil.
2. Arrange the balls into the fryer and cook for 16 minutes at 400 F, until crispy.

Nutrition: Calories 234 Fat 5.2 g Carbs 4.3 g Protein 6.2 g

176. VERMICELLI NOODLES & VEGETABLES ROLLS

PREPARATION TIME
5 MINUTES

COOK TIME
25

SERVING
8

INGREDIENTS

- 8 spring roll wrappers
- 1 cup cooked and cooled vermicelli noodles
- 2 garlic cloves, finely chopped
- 1 tbsp minced fresh ginger
- 2 tbsp soy sauce
- 1 tsp sesame oil
- 1 red bell pepper, seeds removed, chopped
- 1 cup finely chopped mushrooms
- 1 cup finely chopped carrot
- ½ cup finely chopped scallions

DIRECTIONS

1. In a saucepan, add garlic, ginger, soy sauce, pepper, mushroom, carrot and scallions, and stir-fry over high heat for a few minutes, until soft. Add in vermicelli noodles; remove from the heat.
2. Place the spring roll wrappers onto a working board. Spoon the dollops of veggie and noodle mixture at the center of each spring roll wrapper. Roll the spring rolls and tuck the corners and edges in to create neat and secure rolls.
3. Spray with oil and transfer them to the air fryer. Cook for 12 minutes at 340 F, turning once halfway through. Cook until golden and crispy. Serve with soy or sweet chili sauce.

Nutrition: Calories 312 Fat 5 g Carbs 5.4g Protein 3 g

177. BEEF BALLS WITH MIXED HERBS

PREPARATION TIME
5 MINUTES

COOK TIME
25

SERVING
4

INGREDIENTS

- 1 lb. ground beef
- 1 onion, finely chopped
- 3 garlic cloves, finely chopped
- 2 eggs
- 1 cup breadcrumbs
- ½ cup fresh mixed herbs
- 1tbsp mustard
- Salt and black pepper to taste
- Olive oil

DIRECTIONS

1. In a bowl, add beef, onion, garlic, eggs, crumbs, herbs, mustard, salt, and pepper and mix with hands to combine.
2. Shape into balls and arrange them in the air fryer's basket. Drizzle with oil and cook for 16 minutes at 380 F, turning once halfway through.

Nutrition: Calories 315 Fat 5 g Carbs 9 g Protein 8 g

178. ROASTED PUMPKIN SEEDS

PREPARATION TIME
10 MINUTES

COOK TIME
40

SERVING
4

INGREDIENTS

- 1 cup pumpkin seeds, pulp removed, rinsed
- 1 tbsp butter, melted
- 1 tbsp brown sugar
- 1 tsp orange zest
- ½ tsp cardamom
- ½ tsp salt

DIRECTIONS

1. Cook the seeds for 4 minutes at 320 F, in your air fryer, to avoid moisture. In a bowl, whisk melted butter, sugar, zest, cardamom and salt.
2. Add the seeds to the bowl and toss to coat thoroughly.
3. Transfer the seeds to the air fryer and cook for 35 minutes at 300 F, shaking the basket every 10-12 minutes Cook until lightly browned.

Nutrition: Calories 536 Fat 42.86g Calcium: 71g Sodium: 571gp

179. BUTTERY PARMESAN BROCCOLI FLORETS

PREPARATION TIME
5 MINUTES

COOK TIME
20

SERVING
2

INGREDIENTS

- 2 tbsp butter, melted
- 1 egg white
- 1 garlic clove, grated
- ¼ tsp salt
- A pinch of black pepper
- ½ lb. broccoli florets
- ⅓ cup grated Parmesan cheese

DIRECTIONS

1. In a bowl, whisk together the butter, egg, garlic, salt, and black pepper.
2. Toss in broccoli to coat well.
3. Top with Parmesan cheese and; toss to coat.
4. Arrange broccoli in a single layer in the air fryer, without overcrowding.
5. Cook it in batches for 10 minutes at 360 F.
6. Remove to a serving plate and sprinkle with Parmesan cheese.

Nutrition: Calories 350 Fat 27 g Carbs 20g Protein 15 g

180. SPICY CHICKPEAS

PREPARATION TIME
5 MINUTES

COOK TIME
10

SERVING
4

INGREDIENTS

- 1 (15-oz.) can chickpeas rinsed and Dry-out
- 1 tablespoon olive oil
- ½ teaspoon ground cumin
- ½ teaspoon cayenne pepper
- ½ teaspoon smoked paprika
- Salt, as required

DIRECTIONS

1. In a bowl, add all the ingredients and toss to coat well.
2. Press "Power Button" of Air Fry Oven and turn the dial to select the "Air Fry" mode.
3. Press the Time button and again turn the dial to set the cooking time to 10 minutes
4. Now push the Temp button and rotate the dial to set the temperature at 390 degrees F.
5. Press "Start/Pause" button to start.
6. When the unit beeps to show that it is preheated, open the lid.
7. Arrange the chickpeas in "Air Fry Basket" and insert in the oven.
8. Serve warm.

Nutrition: Calories 146 Fat 4.5 g Carbs 18.8 g Protein 6.3 g

181. ROASTED PEANUTS

PREPARATION TIME
5 MINUTES

COOK TIME
14

SERVING
6

INGREDIENTS

- 1½ cups raw peanuts
- Nonstick cooking spray

DIRECTIONS

1. Press "Power Button" of Air Fry Oven and turn the dial to select the "Air Fry" mode. Press the Time button and again turn the dial to set the cooking time to 14 minutes
2. Now push the Temp button and rotate the dial to set the temperature at 320 degrees F. Press "Start/Pause" button to start.
3. When the unit beeps to show that it is preheated, open the lid.
4. Arrange the peanuts in "Air Fry Basket" and insert in the oven.
5. Toss the peanuts twice.
6. After 9 minutes of cooking, spray the peanuts with cooking spray.
7. Serve warm.

Nutrition: Calories 207 Fat 18 g Carbs 5.9 g Protein 9.4 g

182. ROASTED CASHEWS

PREPARATION TIME
5 MINUTES

COOK TIME
5

SERVING
6

INGREDIENTS

- 1½ cups raw cashew nuts
- 1 teaspoon butter, melted
- Salt and freshly ground black pepper, as needed

DIRECTIONS

1. In a bowl, mix together all the ingredients.
2. Press "Power Button" of Air Fry Oven and turn the dial to select the "Air Fry" mode.
3. Press the Time button and again turn the dial to set the cooking time to 5 minutes
4. Now push the Temp button and rotate the dial to set the temperature at 355 degrees F.
5. Press "Start/Pause" button to start.
6. When the unit beeps to show that it is preheated, open the lid.
7. Arrange the cashews in "Air Fry Basket" and insert in the oven.
8. Shake the cashews once halfway through.

Nutrition: Calories 202 Fat 16.5 g Carbs 11.2 g Protein 5.3 g

183. FRENCH FRIES

PREPARATION TIME
15 MINUTES

COOK TIME
30

SERVING
4

INGREDIENTS

- 1 lb. potatoes, peeled and cut into strips
- 3 tablespoons olive oil
- ½ teaspoon onion powder
- ½ teaspoon garlic powder
- 1 teaspoon paprika

DIRECTIONS

1. In a large bowl of water, soak the potato strips for about 1 hour.
2. Dry out the potato strips well and pat them dry with the paper towels.
3. In a large bowl, add the potato strips and the remaining ingredients and toss to coat well.
4. Press "Power Button" of Air Fry Oven and turn the dial to select the "Air Fry" mode.
5. Press the Time button and again turn the dial to set the cooking time to 30 minutes
6. Now push the Temp button and rotate the dial to set the temperature at 375 degrees F.
7. Press "Start/Pause" button to start.
8. When the unit beeps to show that it is preheated, open the lid.
9. Arrange the potato fries in "Air Fry Basket" and insert in the oven.
10. Serve warm.

Nutrition: Calories 172 Fat 10.7 g Carbs 18.6 g Protein 2.1 g

184. ZUCCHINI FRIES

PREPARATION TIME
10 MINUTES

COOK TIME
20

SERVING
4

INGREDIENTS

- 1 lb. zucchini, sliced into 2½-inch sticks
- Salt, as required
- 2 tablespoons olive oil
- ¾ cup panko breadcrumbs

DIRECTIONS

1. In a colander, add the zucchini and sprinkle with salt. Set aside for about 10 minutes. Gently pat dry the zucchini sticks with the paper towels and coat with oil.
2. In a shallow dish, add the breadcrumbs. Coat the zucchini sticks with breadcrumbs evenly.
3. Press "Power Button" of Air Fry Oven and turn the dial to select the "Air Fry" mode.
4. Press the Time button and again turn the dial to set the cooking time to 12 minutes
5. Now push the Temp button and rotate the dial to set the temperature at 400 degrees F.
6. Press "Start/Pause" button to start.
7. When the unit beeps to show that it is preheated, open the lid.
8. Arrange the zucchini fries in "Air Fry Basket" and insert in the oven.
9. Serve warm.

Nutrition: Calories 151 Fat 8.6 g Carbs 6.9 g Protein 1.9 g

185. SPICY CARROT FRIES

PREPARATION TIME
10 MINUTES

COOK TIME
12

SERVING
2

INGREDIENTS

- 1 large carrot, peeled and cut into sticks
- 1 tablespoon fresh rosemary, chopped finely
- 1 tablespoon olive oil
- ¼ teaspoon cayenne pepper
- Salt and ground black pepper, as required

DIRECTIONS

1. In a bowl, add all the ingredients and mix well. Press "Power Button" of Air Fry Oven and turn the dial to select the "Air Fry" mode.
2. Press the Time button and again turn the dial to set the cooking time to 12 minutes
3. Now push the Temp button and rotate the dial to set the temperature at 390 degrees F.
4. Press "Start/Pause" button to start.
5. When the unit beeps to show that it is preheated, open the lid.
6. Arrange the carrot fries in "Air Fry Basket" and insert in the oven.
7. Serve warm.

Nutrition: Calories 81 Fat 8.3 g Carbs 4.7 g Protein 0.4 g

186. CINNAMON CARROT FRIES

PREPARATION TIME
10 MINUTES

COOK TIME
12

SERVING
6

INGREDIENTS

- 1 lb. carrots, peeled and cut into sticks
- 1 teaspoon maple syrup
- 1 teaspoon olive oil
- ½ teaspoon ground cinnamon
- Salt, to taste

DIRECTIONS

1. In a bowl, add all the ingredients and mix well.
2. Press "Power Button" of Air Fry Oven and turn the dial to select the "Air Fry" mode. Press the Time button and again turn the dial to set the cooking time to 12 minutes
3. Now push the Temp button and rotate the dial to set the temperature at 400 degrees F.
4. Press "Start/Pause" button to start.
5. When the unit beeps to show that it is preheated, open the lid.
6. Arrange the carrot fries in "Air Fry Basket" and insert in the oven.
7. Serve warm.

Nutrition: Calories 41 Fat 0.8 g Carbs 8.3 g Protein 0.6 g

187. SQUASH FRIES

PREPARATION TIME
10 MINUTES

COOK TIME
35

SERVING
2

INGREDIENTS

- 14 oz. butternut squash, peeled, seeded and cut into strips
- 2 teaspoons olive oil
- ½ teaspoon ground cinnamon
- ½ teaspoon red chili powder
- ¼ teaspoon garlic salt
- Salt and freshly ground black pepper, as needed

DIRECTIONS

1. In a bowl, add all the ingredients and toss to coat well. Press "Power Button" of Air Fry Oven and turn the dial to select the "Air Fry" mode.
2. Press the Time button and again turn the dial to set the cooking time to 30 minutes. Now push the Temp button and rotate the dial to set the temperature at 400 degrees F.
3. Press "Start/Pause" button to start. When the unit beeps to show that it is preheated, open the lid.
4. Arrange the squash fries in "Air Fry Basket" and insert in the oven.
5. Serve warm.

Nutrition: Calories 134 Fat 5 g Carbs 24.3 g Protein 2.1 g

188. AVOCADO VEGETABLE FRIES

PREPARATION TIME
15 MINUTES

COOK TIME
7

SERVING
2

INGREDIENTS

- ¼ cup all-purpose flour
- Salt and freshly ground black pepper, as needed
- 1 egg 1 teaspoon water
- ½ cup panko breadcrumbs
- 1 avocado, peeled, pitted and sliced into 8 pieces
- Non-stick cooking spray

DIRECTIONS

1. In a shallow bowl, mix together the flour, salt, and black pepper.
2. In a second bowl, mix well egg and water.
3. In a third bowl, put the breadcrumbs.
4. Coat the avocado slices with flour mixture, then dip into egg mixture and finally, coat evenly with the breadcrumbs.
5. Now, spray the avocado slices evenly with cooking spray.
6. Press "Power Button" of Air Fry Oven and turn the dial to select the "Air Fry" mode.
7. Press the Time button and again turn the dial to set the cooking time to 7 minutes
8. Now push the Temp button and rotate the dial to set the temperature at 400 degrees F.
9. Press "Start/Pause" button to start.
10. When the unit beeps to show that it is preheated, open the lid.
11. Arrange the avocado fries in "Air Fry Basket" and insert in the oven.
12. Serve warm.

Nutrition: Calories 340 Fat 14 g Carbs 30 g Protein 23 g

189. DILL PICKLE FRIES

PREPARATION TIME
15 MINUTES

COOK TIME
15

SERVING
8

INGREDIENTS

- 1 (16-oz.) jar spicy dill pickle spears Dry out and pat dried
- ¾ cup all-purpose flour
- ½ teaspoon paprika
- 1 egg, beaten
- ¼ cup milk
- 1 cup panko breadcrumbs
- Nonstick cooking spray

DIRECTIONS

1. In a shallow dish, mix together the flour, and paprika.
2. In a second dish, place the milk and egg and mix well.
3. In a third dish, put the breadcrumbs.
4. Coat the pickle spears with flour mixture, then dip into egg mixture and finally, coat evenly with the breadcrumbs.
5. Now, spray the pickle spears evenly with cooking spray.
6. Press "Power Button" of Air Fry Oven and turn the dial to select the "Air Fry" mode.
7. Press the Time button and again turn the dial to set the cooking time to 15 minutes
8. Now push the Temp button and rotate the dial to set the temperature at 400 degrees F.
9. Press "Start/Pause" button to start. When the unit beeps to show that it is preheated, open the lid.
10. Arrange the squash fries in "Air Fry Basket" and insert in the oven.
11. Serve warm.
12. Flip the fries once halfway through.
13. Serve warm.

Nutrition: Calories 110 Fat 1.9 g Carbs 12.8 g Protein 2.7 g

190. MOZZARELLA STICKS

PREPARATION TIME
15 MINUTES

COOK TIME
12

SERVING
3

INGREDIENTS

- ¼ cup white flour
- 2 eggs
- 3 tablespoons nonfat milk
- 1 cup plain breadcrumbs
- 1 lb. Mozzarella cheese block cut into 3x½-inch sticks

DIRECTIONS

1. In a shallow dish, add the flour.
2. In a second shallow dish, mix together the eggs, and milk.
3. In a third shallow dish, place the breadcrumbs.
4. Coat the Mozzarella sticks with flour, then dip into egg mixture and finally, coat evenly with the breadcrumbs.
5. Press "Power Button" of Air Fry Oven and turn the dial to select the "Air Fry" mode.
6. Press the Time button and again turn the dial to set the cooking time to 12 minutes
7. Now push the Temp button and rotate the dial to set the temperature at 400 degrees F.
8. Press "Start/Pause" button to start.
9. When the unit beeps to show that it is preheated, open the lid.
10. Arrange the mozzarella sticks in "Air Fry Basket" and insert in the oven.
11. Serve warm

Nutrition: Calories 254 Fat 6.6 g Carbs 35.2 g Protein 12.8 g

191. TORTILLA CHIPS

PREPARATION TIME
10 MINUTES

COOK TIME
3

SERVING
3

INGREDIENTS

- 4 corn tortillas cut into triangles
- 1 tablespoon olive oil
- Salt, to taste

DIRECTIONS

1. Coat the tortilla chips with oi and then, sprinkle each side of the tortillas with salt.
2. Press "Power Button" of Air Fry Oven and turn the dial to select the "Air Fry" mode.
3. Press the Time button and again turn the dial to set the cooking time to 3 minutes.
4. Now push the Temp button and rotate the dial to set the temperature at 390 degrees F.
5. Press "Start/Pause" button to start.
6. When the unit beeps to show that it is preheated, open the lid.
7. Arrange the tortilla chips in "Air Fry Basket" and insert in the oven.
8. Serve warm.

Nutrition: Calories 110 Fat 5.6 g Carbs 14.3 g Protein 1.8 g

192. FLAX SEED CHIPS

PREPARATION TIME
5 MINUTES

COOK TIME
15

SERVING
4

INGREDIENTS

- 1 Cup almond flour
- 1/2 Cup flax seeds
- 1 1/2 Teaspoons seasoned salt
- 1 Teaspoon sea salt
- 1/2 Cup water

DIRECTIONS

1. Preheat the Air fryer toaster oven to 170 degrees C. Combine almond flour, flax seeds, 1 1/2 teaspoons seasoned salt and sea salt in a container; Stir in the water up to the dough is completely mixed. Shape the dough into narrow size slices the size of a bite and place them on a baking sheet. Sprinkle the rounds with seasoned salt. Bake in preheated air fryer toaster oven up to crispy, about 15 minutes. Cool fully and store in an airtight box or in a sealed bag.

Nutrition: Calories 126.9 Fat 6.1g Carbs 15.9 g Protein 2.9g

193. SALTED HAZELNUTS

PREPARATION TIME
15 MINUTES

COOK TIME
10

SERVING
8

INGREDIENTS

- Cups dry roasted Hazelnuts, no salt added
- Tablespoons coconut oil
- 1 Teaspoon garlic powder
- 1 Sprig fresh Thyme, chopped
- 1 1/2 Teaspoons salt

DIRECTIONS

1. Preheat the Air fryer toaster oven to 175 ° C. Mix the Hazelnuts, coconut oil, garlic powder and thyme in a bowl until the nuts are fully covered. Sprinkle with salt. Spread evenly on a baking sheet. Bake in the preheated Air fryer toaster oven for 10 minutes.

Nutrition: Calories 237 Fat 21.3 g Carbs 5.9 g Protein 7.4g

194. BAGUETTE BREAD

PREPARATION TIME
15 MINUTES

COOK TIME
20

SERVING
8

INGREDIENTS

- ¾ cup warm water
- ¾ teaspoon quick yeast
- ½ teaspoon demerara sugar
- 1 cup bread flour
- ½ cup whole-wheat flour
- ½ cup oat flour
- 1¼ teaspoons salt

DIRECTIONS

1. In a large bowl, place the water and sprinkle with yeast and sugar.
2. Set aside for 5 minutes or until foamy.
3. Add the bread flour and salt mix until a stiff dough form.
4. Put the dough onto a floured surface and with your hands, knead until smooth and elastic.
5. Now, shape the dough into a ball.
6. Place the dough into a slightly oiled bowl and turn to coat well.
7. With a plastic wrap, cover the bowl and place in a warm place for about 1 hour or until doubled in size.
8. With your hands, punch down the dough and form into a long slender loaf.
9. Place the loaf onto a lightly greased baking sheet and set aside in warm place, uncovered, for about 30 minutes
10. Press "Power Button" of Air Fry Oven and turn the dial to select the "Air Bake" mode.
11. Press the Time button and again turn the dial to set the cooking time to 20 minutes
12. Now push the Temp button and rotate the dial to set the temperature at 450 degrees F.
13. Press "Start/Pause" button to start.
14. When the unit beeps to show that it is preheated, open the lid.
15. Carefully, arrange the dough onto the "Wire Rack" and insert in the oven.
16. Carefully, invert the bread onto wire rack to cool completely before slicing.
17. Cut the bread into desired-sized slices and serve.

Nutrition: Calories 114 Fat 0.8 g Carbs 22.8 g Protein 3.8 g

195. YOGURT BREAD

PREPARATION TIME 20 MINUTES

COOK TIME 40

SERVING 10

INGREDIENTS

- 1½ cups warm water, divided
- 1½ teaspoons active dry yeast
- 1 teaspoon sugar
- 3 cups all-purpose flour
- 1 cup plain Greek yogurt
- 2 teaspoons kosher salt

DIRECTIONS

1. Add ½ cup of the warm water, yeast and sugar in the bowl of a stand mixer, fitted with the dough hook attachment and mix well.
2. Set aside for about 5 minutes
3. Add the flour, yogurt, and salt and mix on medium-low speed until the dough comes together.
4. Then, mix on medium speed for 5 minutes
5. Place the dough into a bowl.
6. With a plastic wrap, cover the bowl and place in a warm place for about 2-3 hours or until doubled in size.
7. Transfer the dough onto a lightly floured surface and shape into a smooth ball.
8. Place the dough onto a greased parchment paper-lined rack.
9. With a kitchen towel, cover the dough and let rest for 15 minutes
10. With a very sharp knife, cut a 4x½-inch deep cut down the center of the dough.
11. Press "Power Button" of Air Fry Oven and turn the dial to select the "Air Roast" mode.
12. Press the Time button and again turn the dial to set the cooking time to 40 minutes
13. Now push the Temp button and rotate the dial to set the temperature at 325 degrees F.
14. Press "Start/Pause" button to start.
15. When the unit beeps to show that it is preheated, open the lid.
16. Carefully, arrange the dough onto the "Wire Rack" and insert in the oven.
17. Carefully, invert the bread onto wire rack to cool completely before slicing.
18. Cut the bread into desired-sized slices and serve.

Nutrition: Calories 157 Fat 0.7 g Carbs 31 g Protein 5.5 g

196. SUNFLOWER SEED BREAD

PREPARATION TIME
15 MINUTES

COOK TIME
18

SERVING
6

INGREDIENTS

- 2/3 cup whole-wheat flour
- 2/3 cup plain flour
- 1/3 cup sunflower seeds
- ½ sachet instant yeast
- 1 teaspoon salt
- 2/3-1 cup lukewarm water

DIRECTIONS

1. In a bowl, mix together the flours, sunflower seeds, yeast, and salt.
2. Slowly, add in the water, stirring continuously until a soft dough ball form.
3. Now, move the dough onto a lightly floured surface and knead for about 5 minutes using your hands.
4. Make a ball from the dough and place into a bowl.
5. With a plastic wrap, cover the bowl and place at a warm place for about 30 minutes
6. Grease a cake pan.
7. Coat the top of dough with water and place into the prepared cake pan.
8. Press "Power Button" of Air Fry Oven and turn the dial to select the "Air Crisp" mode.
9. Press the Time button and again turn the dial to set the cooking time to 18 minutes
10. Now push the Temp button and rotate the dial to set the temperature at 390 degrees F.
11. Press "Start/Pause" button to start.
12. When the unit beeps to show that it is preheated, open the lid.
13. Arrange the pan in "Air Fry Basket" and insert in the oven.
14. Place the pan onto a wire rack to cool for about 10 minutes
15. Carefully, invert the bread onto wire rack to cool completely before slicing.
16. Cut the bread into desired-sized slices and serve.

Nutrition: Calories 132 Fat 1.7 g Carbs 24.4 g Protein 4.9 g

197. DATE BREAD

PREPARATION TIME
15 MINUTES

COOK TIME
22

SERVING
10

INGREDIENTS

- 2½ cup dates, pitted and chopped
- ¼ cup butter
- 1 cup hot water
- 1½ cups flour
- ½ cup brown sugar
- 1 teaspoon baking powder
- 1 teaspoon baking soda
- ½ teaspoon salt
- 1 egg

DIRECTIONS

1. In a large bowl, add the dates, butter and top with the hot water.
2. Set aside for about 5 minutes
3. In another bowl, mix together the flour, brown sugar, baking powder, baking soda, and salt.
4. In the same bowl of dates, mix well the flour mixture, and egg.
5. Grease a baking pan.
6. Place the mixture into the prepared pan.
7. Press "Power Button" of Air Fry Oven and turn the dial to select the "Air Crisp" mode.
8. Press the Time button and again turn the dial to set the cooking time to 22 minutes
9. Now push the Temp button and rotate the dial to set the temperature at 340 degrees F.
10. Press "Start/Pause" button to start.
11. When the unit beeps to show that it is preheated, open the lid.
12. Arrange the pan in "Air Fry Basket" and insert in the oven.
13. Place the pan onto a wire rack to cool for about 10 minutes
14. Carefully, invert the bread onto wire rack to cool completely before slicing.
15. Cut the bread into desired-sized slices and serve.

Nutrition: Calories 269 Fat 5.4 g Carbs 55.1 g Protein 3.6 g

198. DATE & WALNUT BREAD

PREPARATION TIME
15 MINUTES

COOK TIME
35

SERVING
5

INGREDIENTS

- 1 cup dates, pitted and sliced
- ¾ cup walnuts, chopped
- 1 tablespoon instant coffee powder
- 1 tablespoon hot water
- 1¼ cups plain flour
- ¼ teaspoon salt
- ½ teaspoon baking powder
- ½ teaspoon baking soda
- ½ cup condensed milk
- ½ cup butter, softened
- ½ teaspoon vanilla essence

DIRECTIONS

1. In a large bowl, add the dates, butter and top with the hot water.
2. Set aside for about 30 minutes
3. Dry out well and set aside.
4. In a small bowl, add the coffee powder and hot water and mix well.
5. In a large bowl, mix together the flour, baking powder, baking soda and salt.
6. In another large bowl, add the condensed milk and butter and beat until smooth.
7. Add the flour mixture, coffee mixture and vanilla essence and mix until well combined.
8. Fold in dates and ½ cup of walnut.
9. Line a baking pan with a lightly greased parchment paper.
10. Place the mixture into the prepared pan and sprinkle with the remaining walnuts.
11. Press "Power Button" of Air Fry Oven and turn the dial to select the "Air Crisp" mode.
12. Press the Time button and again turn the dial to set the cooking time to 35 minutes
13. Now push the Temp button and rotate the dial to set the temperature at 320 degrees F.
14. Press "Start/Pause" button to start.
15. When the unit beeps to show that it is preheated, open the lid.
16. Arrange the pan in "Air Fry Basket" and insert in the oven.
17. Place the pan onto a wire rack to cool for about 10 minutes
18. Carefully, invert the bread onto wire rack to cool completely before slicing.
19. Cut the bread into desired-sized slices and serve.

Nutrition: Calories 593 Fat 32.6 g Carbs 69.4 g Protein 11.2 g

199. BROWN SUGAR BANANA BREAD

PREPARATION TIME
15 MINUTES

COOK TIME
30

SERVING
4

INGREDIENTS

- 1 egg
- 1 ripe banana, peeled and mashed
- ¼ cup milk
- 2 tablespoons canola oil
- 2 tablespoons brown sugar
- ¾ cup plain flour
- ½ teaspoon baking soda

DIRECTIONS

1. Line a very small baking pan with a greased parchment paper.
2. In a small bowl, add the egg and banana and beat well.
3. Add the milk, oil and sugar and beat until well combined.
4. Add the flour and baking soda and mix until just combined.
5. Place the mixture into prepared pan.
6. Press "Power Button" of Air Fry Oven and turn the dial to select the "Air Crisp" mode.
7. Press the Time button and again turn the dial to set the cooking time to 30 minutes
8. Now push the Temp button and rotate the dial to set the temperature at 320 degrees F.
9. Press "Start/Pause" button to start.
10. When the unit beeps to show that it is preheated, open the lid.
11. Arrange the pan in "Air Fry Basket" and insert in the oven.
12. Place the pan onto a wire rack to cool for about 10 minutes
13. Carefully, invert the bread onto wire rack to cool completely before slicing.
14. Cut the bread into desired-sized slices and serve.

Nutrition: Calories 214 Fat 8.7 g Carbs 29.9 g Protein 4.6 g

200. CINNAMON BANANA BREAD

PREPARATION TIME
15 MINUTES

COOK TIME
20

SERVING
8

INGREDIENTS

- 1 1/3 cups flour
- 2/3 cup sugar
- 1 teaspoon baking soda
- 1 teaspoon baking powder
- 1 teaspoon ground cinnamon
- 1 teaspoon salt
- ½ cup milk
- ½ cup olive oil
- 3 bananas, peeled and sliced

DIRECTIONS

1. In the bowl of a stand mixer, add all the ingredients and mix well.
2. Grease a loaf pan.
3. Place the mixture into the prepared pan.
4. Press "Power Button" of Air Fry Oven and turn the dial to select the "Air Crisp" mode.
5. Press the Time button and again turn the dial to set the cooking time to 20 minutes
6. Now push the Temp button and rotate the dial to set the temperature at 330 degrees F.
7. Press "Start/Pause" button to start.
8. When the unit beeps to show that it is preheated, open the lid.
9. Arrange the pan in "Air Fry Basket" and insert in the oven.
10. Place the pan onto a wire rack to cool for about 10 minutes
11. Carefully, invert the bread onto wire rack to cool completely before slicing.
12. Cut the bread into desired-sized slices and serve.

Nutrition: Calories 295 Fat 13.3g Carbs 44 g Protein 3.1 g

201. BANANA & WALNUT BREAD

PREPARATION TIME
15 MINUTES

COOK TIME
25

SERVING
10

INGREDIENTS

- 1½ cups self-rising flour
- ¼ teaspoon bicarbonate of soda
- 5 tablespoons plus 1 teaspoon butter
- 2/3 cup plus ½ tablespoon caster sugar
- 2 medium eggs
- 3½ oz. walnuts, chopped
- 2 cups bananas, peeled and mashed

DIRECTIONS

1. In a bowl, mix together the flour and bicarbonate of soda.
2. In another bowl, add the butter, and sugar and beat until pale and fluffy.
3. Add the eggs, one at a time along with a little flour and mix well.
4. Stir in the remaining flour and walnuts.
5. Add the bananas and mix until well combined.
6. Grease a loaf pan.
7. Place the mixture into the prepared pan.
8. Press "Power Button" of Air Fry Oven and turn the dial to select the "Air Crisp" mode.
9. Press the Time button and again turn the dial to set the cooking time to 10 minutes
10. Now push the Temp button and rotate the dial to set the temperature at 355 degrees F.
11. Press "Start/Pause" button to start.
12. When the unit beeps to show that it is preheated, open the lid.
13. Arrange the pan in "Air Fry Basket" and insert in the oven.
14. After 10 minutes of cooking, set the temperature at 338 degrees F for 15 minutes
15. Place the pan onto a wire rack to cool for about 10 minutes
16. Carefully, invert the bread onto wire rack to cool completely before slicing.
17. Cut the bread into desired-sized slices and serve.

Nutrition: Calories 270 Fat 12.8 g Carbs 35.5 g Protein 5.8 g

202. BANANA & RAISIN BREAD

PREPARATION TIME
15MINUTES

COOK TIME
40

SERVING
6

INGREDIENTS

- 1½ cups cake flour
- 1 teaspoon baking soda
- ½ teaspoon ground cinnamon
- Salt, to taste
- ½ cup vegetable oil
- 2 eggs
- ½ cup sugar
- ½ teaspoon vanilla extract
- 3 medium bananas, peeled and mashed
- ½ cup raisins, chopped finely

DIRECTIONS

1. In a large bowl, mix together the flour, baking soda, cinnamon, and salt.
2. In another bowl, beat well eggs and oil.
3. Add the sugar, vanilla extract, and bananas and beat until well combined.
4. Add the flour mixture and stir until just combined.
5. Place the mixture into a lightly greased baking pan and sprinkle with raisins.
6. With a piece of foil, cover the pan loosely.
7. Press "Power Button" of Air Fry Oven and turn the dial to select the "Air Bake" mode.
8. Press the Time button and again turn the dial to set the cooking time to 30 minutes
9. Now push the Temp button and rotate the dial to set the temperature at 300 degrees F.
10. Press "Start/Pause" button to start.
11. When the unit beeps to show that it is preheated, open the lid.
12. Arrange the pan in "Air Fry Basket" and insert in the oven.
13. After 30 minutes of cooking, set the temperature to 285 degrees F for 10 minutes
14. Place the pan onto a wire rack to cool for about 10 minutes
15. Carefully, invert the bread onto wire rack to cool completely before slicing.
16. Cut the bread into desired-sized slices and serve.

Nutrition: Calories 448 Fat 20.2 g Carbs 63.9 g Protein 6.1 g

203. 3-INGREDIENTS BANANA BREAD

PREPARATION TIME
10 MINUTES

COOK TIME
20

SERVING
6

INGREDIENTS

- 2 (6.4-oz.) banana muffin mix
- 1 cup water
- 1 ripe banana, peeled and mashed

DIRECTIONS

1. In a bowl, add all the ingredients and with a whisk, mix until well combined.
2. Place the mixture into a lightly greased loaf pan.
3. Press "Power Button" of Air Fry Oven and turn the dial to select the "Air Bake" mode.
4. Press the Time button and again turn the dial to set the cooking time to 20 minutes
5. Now push the Temp button and rotate the dial to set the temperature at 360 degrees F.
6. Press "Start/Pause" button to start.
7. When the unit beeps to show that it is preheated, open the lid.
8. Arrange the pan in "Air Fry Basket" and insert in the oven.
9. Place the pan onto a wire rack to cool for about 10 minutes
10. Carefully, invert the bread onto wire rack to cool completely before slicing.
11. Cut the bread into desired-sized slices and serve.

Nutrition: Calories 144 Fat 3.8 g Carbs 25.5 g Protein 1.9 g

204. YOGURT BANANA BREAD

PREPARATION TIME
15 MINUTES

COOK TIME
28

SERVING
5

INGREDIENTS

- 1 medium very ripe banana, peeled and mashed
- 1 large egg
- 1 tablespoon canola oil
- 1 tablespoon plain Greek yogurt
- ¼ teaspoon pure vanilla extract
- ½ cup all-purpose flour
- ¼ cup granulated white sugar
- ¼ teaspoon ground cinnamon
- ¼ teaspoon baking soda
- 1/8 teaspoon sea salt

DIRECTIONS

1. In a bowl, add the mashed banana, egg, oil, yogurt and vanilla and beat until well combined.
2. Add the flour, sugar, baking soda, cinnamon and salt and mix until just combined.
3. Place the mixture into a lightly greased mini loaf pan.
4. Press "Power Button" of Air Fry Oven and turn the dial to select the "Air Bake" mode.
5. Press the Time button and again turn the dial to set the cooking time to 28 minutes
6. Now push the Temp button and rotate the dial to set the temperature at 350 degrees F.
7. Press "Start/Pause" button to start.
8. When the unit beeps to show that it is preheated, open the lid.
9. Arrange the pan in "Air Fry Basket" and insert in the oven.
10. Place the pan onto a wire rack to cool for about 10 minutes
11. Carefully, invert the bread onto wire rack to cool completely before slicing.
12. Cut the bread into desired-sized slices and serve.

Nutrition: Calories 145 Fat 4 g Carbs 25 g Protein 3 g

205. SOUR CREAM BANANA BREAD

PREPARATION TIME
15 MINUTES

COOK TIME
37

SERVING
8

INGREDIENTS

- ¾ cup all-purpose flour
- ¼ teaspoon baking soda
- ¼ teaspoon salt
- 2 ripe bananas, peeled and mashed
- ½ cup granulated sugar
- ¼ cup sour cream
- ¼ cup vegetable oil
- 1 large egg
- ½ teaspoon pure vanilla extract

DIRECTIONS

1. In a large bowl, mix together the flour, baking soda and salt.
2. In another bowl, add the bananas, egg, sugar, sour cream, oil and vanilla and beat until well combined.
3. Add the flour mixture and mix until just combined.
4. Place the mixture into a lightly greased pan. Press "Power Button" of Air Fry Oven and turn the dial to select the "Air Crisp" mode.
5. Press the Time button and again turn the dial to set the cooking time to 37 minutes
6. Now push the Temp button and rotate the dial to set the temperature at 310 degrees F. Press "Start/Pause" button to start.
7. When the unit beeps to show that it is preheated, open the lid. Arrange the pan in "Air Fry Basket" and insert in the oven.
8. Place the pan onto a wire rack to cool for about 10 minutes
9. Carefully, invert the bread onto wire rack to cool completely before slicing.
10. Cut the bread into desired-sized slices and serve.

Nutrition: Calories 201 Fat 9.2g Carbs 28.6g Protein 2.6g

206. PEANUT BUTTER BANANA BREAD

PREPARATION TIME
15 MINUTES

COOK TIME
40

SERVING
6

INGREDIENTS

- 1 cup plus 1 tablespoon all-purpose flour
- ¼ teaspoon baking soda
- 1 teaspoon baking powder
- ¼ teaspoon salt
- 1 large egg
- 1/3 cup granulated sugar
- ¼ cup canola oil
- 2 tablespoons creamy peanut butter
- 2 tablespoons sour cream
- 1 teaspoon vanilla extract
- 2 medium ripe bananas, peeled and mashed
- ¾ cup walnuts, roughly chopped

DIRECTIONS

1. In a bowl and mix the flour, baking powder, baking soda, and salt together.
2. In another large bowl, add the egg, sugar, oil, peanut butter, sour cream, and vanilla extract and beat until well combined.
3. Add the bananas and beat until well combined.
4. Add the flour mixture and mix until just combined.
5. Gently, fold in the walnuts.
6. Place the mixture into a lightly greased pan.
7. Press "Power Button" of Air Fry Oven and turn the dial to select the "Air Crisp" mode.
8. Press the Time button and again turn the dial to set the cooking time to 40 minutes
9. Now push the Temp button and rotate the dial to set the temperature at 330 degrees F.
10. Press "Start/Pause" button to start.
11. When the unit beeps to show that it is preheated, open the lid.
12. Arrange the pan in "Air Fry Basket" and insert in the oven.
13. Place the pan onto a wire rack to cool for about 10 minutes
14. Carefully, invert the bread onto wire rack to cool completely before slicing.
15. Cut the bread into desired-sized slices and serve.

Nutrition: Calories 384 Fat 23 g Carbs 39.3 g Protein 8.9 g

207. CHOCOLATE BANANA BREAD

PREPARATION TIME 15 MINUTES

COOK TIME 20

SERVING 8

INGREDIENTS

- 2 cups flour
- ½ teaspoon baking soda
- ½ teaspoon baking powder
- ½ teaspoon salt
- ¾ cup sugar
- 1/3 cup butter, softened
- 3 eggs
- 1 tablespoon vanilla extract
- 1 cup milk
- ½ cup bananas, peeled and mashed
- 1 cup chocolate chips

DIRECTIONS

1. In a bowl, mix together the flour, baking soda, baking powder, and salt.
2. In another large bowl, add the butter, and sugar and beat until light and fluffy.
3. Add the eggs, and vanilla extract and whisk until well combined.
4. Add the flour mixture and mix until well combined.
5. Add the milk, and mashed bananas and mix well.
6. Gently, fold in the chocolate chips. Place the mixture into a lightly greased loaf pan.
7. Press "Power Button" of Air Fry Oven and turn the dial to select the "Air Crisp" mode.
8. Press the Time button and again turn the dial to set the cooking time to 20 minutes
9. Now push the Temp button and rotate the dial to set the temperature at 360 degrees F.
10. Press "Start/Pause" button to start. When the unit beeps to show that it is preheated, open the lid.
11. Arrange the pan in "Air Fry Basket" and insert in the oven.
12. Place the pan onto a wire rack to cool for about 10 minutes Carefully, invert the bread onto wire rack to cool completely before slicing.
13. Cut the bread into desired-sized slices and serve.

Nutrition: Calories 416 Fat 16.5 g Carbs 59.2 g Protein 8.1 g

208. ALLSPICE CHICKEN WINGS

PREPARATION TIME
- MINUTES

COOK TIME
45

SERVING
8

INGREDIENTS

- ½ tsp celery salt
- ½ tsp bay leaf powder
- ½ tsp ground black pepper
- ½ tsp paprika
- ¼ tsp dry mustard
- ¼ tsp cayenne pepper
- ¼ tsp allspice
- 2 pounds chicken wings

DIRECTIONS

1. Grease the air fryer basket and preheat to 340 F. In a bowl, mix celery salt, bay leaf powder, black pepper, paprika, dry mustard, cayenne pepper, and allspice. Coat the wings thoroughly in this mixture.
2. Arrange the wings in an even layer in the basket of the air fryer. Cook the chicken until it's no longer pinks around the bone, for 30 minutes then, increase the temperature to 380 F and cook for 6 minutes more, until crispy on the outside.

Nutrition: Calories 332 Fat 10.1 g Carbs 31.3 g Protein 12 g

209. FRIDAY NIGHT PINEAPPLE STICKY RIBS

PREPARATION TIME
10 MINUTES

COOK TIME
20

SERVING
4

INGREDIENTS

- 2 lb. cut spareribs
- 7 oz salad dressing
- 1 (5-oz) can pineapple juice
- 2 cups water
- Garlic salt to taste
- Salt and black pepper

DIRECTIONS

1. Sprinkle the ribs with salt and pepper, and place them in a saucepan. Pour water and cook the ribs for 12 minutes on high heat.
2. Dry out the ribs and arrange them in the fryer; sprinkle with garlic salt. Cook it for 15 minutes at 390 F.
3. Prepare the sauce by combining the salad dressing and the pineapple juice. Serve the ribs drizzled with the sauce.

Nutrition: Calories 316 Fat 3.1 g Carbs 1.9 g Protein 5 g

210. EGG ROLL WRAPPED WITH CABBAGE AND PRAWNS

PREPARATION TIME
10 MINUTES

COOK TIME
40

SERVING
4

INGREDIENTS

- 2 tbsp vegetable oil
- 1-inch piece fresh ginger, grated
- 1 tbsp minced garlic
- 1 carrot, cut into strips
- ¼ cup chicken broth
- 2 tbsp reduced-sodium soy sauce
- 1 tbsp sugar
- 1 cup shredded Napa cabbage
- 1 tbsp sesame oil
- 8 cooked prawns, minced
- 1 egg
- 8 egg roll wrappers

DIRECTIONS

1. In a skillet over high heat, heat vegetable oil, and cook ginger and garlic for 40 seconds, until fragrant. Stir in carrot and cook for another 2 minutes Pour in chicken broth, soy sauce, and sugar and bring to a boil.
2. Add cabbage and let simmer until softened, for 4 minutes Remove skillet from the heat and stir in sesame oil. Let cool for 15 minutes Strain cabbage mixture, and fold in minced prawns. Whisk an egg in a small bowl. Fill each egg roll wrapper with prawn mixture, arranging the mixture just below the center of the wrapper.
3. Fold the bottom part over the filling and tuck under. Fold in both sides and tightly roll up. Use the whisked egg to seal the wrapper. Repeat until all egg rolls are ready. Place the rolls into a greased air fryer basket, spray them with oil and cook for 12 minutes at 370 F, turning once halfway through.

Nutrition: Calories 215 Fat 7.9 g Carbs 6.7 g Protein 8 g

211. SESAME GARLIC CHICKEN WINGS

PREPARATION TIME
10 MINUTES

COOK TIME
40

SERVING
4

INGREDIENTS

- 1-pound chicken wings
- 1 cup soy sauce, divided
- ½ cup brown sugar
- ½ cup apple cider vinegar
- 2 tbsp fresh ginger, minced
- 2 tbsp fresh garlic, minced
- 1 tsp finely ground black pepper
- 2 tbsp cornstarch
- 2 tbsp cold water
- 1 tsp sesame seeds

DIRECTIONS

1. In a bowl, add chicken wings, and pour in half cup soy sauce. Refrigerate for 20 minutes; Dry out and pat dry. Arrange the wings in the air fryer and cook for 30 minutes at 380 F, turning once halfway through. Make sure you check them towards the end to avoid overcooking.
2. In a skillet and over medium heat, stir sugar, half cup soy sauce, vinegar, ginger, garlic, and black pepper. Cook until sauce has reduced slightly, about 4 to 6 minutes
3. Dissolve 2 tbsp of cornstarch in cold water, in a bowl, and stir in the slurry into the sauce, until it thickens, for 2 minutes Pour the sauce over wings and sprinkle with sesame seeds.

Nutrition: Calories 413 Fat 8.3 g Carbs 7 g Protein 8.3 g

212. SAVORY CHICKEN NUGGETS WITH PARMESAN CHEESE

PREPARATION TIME
5 MINUTES

COOK TIME
20

SERVING
4

INGREDIENTS

- 1 lb. chicken breast, boneless, skinless, cubed
- ½ tsp ground black pepper
- ¼ tsp kosher salt
- ¼ tsp seasoned salt
- 2 tbsp olive oil
- 5 tbsp plain breadcrumbs
- 2 tbsp panko breadcrumbs
- 2 tbsp grated Parmesan cheese

DIRECTIONS

1. Preheat the air fryer to 380 F and grease. Season the chicken with pepper, kosher salt, and seasoned salt; set aside. In a bowl, pour olive oil. In a separate bowl, add crumb, and Parmesan cheese.
2. Place the chicken pieces in the oil to coat, then dip into breadcrumb mixture, and transfer to the air fryer. Work in batches if needed. Lightly spray chicken with cooking spray.
3. Cook the chicken for 10 minutes, flipping once halfway through. Cook until golden brown on the outside and no pinker on the inside.

Nutrition: Calories 312 Fat 8.9 g Carbs 7 g Protein 10 g

8. VEGETABLES

213. FLAVORED ASPARAGUS

PREPARATION TIME
5 MINUTES

COOK TIME
30

SERVING
2

INGREDIENTS

- Nutritional yeast
- Olive oil non-stick spray
- One bunch of asparagus

DIRECTIONS

1. Wash asparagus and then cut off the bushy, woody ends. Drizzle asparagus with olive oil spray and sprinkle with yeast. In your air fryer, lay asparagus in a singular layer. Cook 8 minutes at 360 degrees.

Nutrition: Calories: 17 Cal Fat: 4 g Carbs: 32 g Protein: 24 g

214. AVOCADO FRIES

PREPARATION TIME
5 MINUTES

COOK TIME
5

SERVING
6

INGREDIENTS

- 1 avocado
- ½ tsp. salt
- ½ C. panko breadcrumbs
- Bean liquid (aquafaba) from a 15-ounce can of white or garbanzo beans

DIRECTIONS

1. Peel, pit, and slice up avocado. Toss salt and breadcrumbs together in a bowl. Place aquafaba into another bowl. Dredge slices of avocado first in aquafaba and then in panko, making sure you get an even coating. Place coated avocado slices into a single layer in the air fryer. Cook 5 minutes at 390 degrees, shaking at 5 minutes. Serve with your favorite keto dipping sauce!

Nutrition: Calories: 102 Fat: 22g Protein: 9g Sugar: 1g

215. SPAGHETTI SQUASH TOTS

PREPARATION TIME
5 MINUTES

COOK TIME
15

SERVING
10

INGREDIENTS

- ¼ tsp. pepper
- ½ tsp. salt
- 1 thinly sliced scallion
- 1 spaghetti squash

DIRECTIONS

1. Wash and cut the squash in lengthwise. Scrape out the seeds. With a fork, remove spaghetti meat by strands and throw out skins. In a clean towel, toss in squash and wring out as much moisture as possible.
2. Place in a bowl and with a knife slice through meat a few times to cut up smaller. Add pepper, salt, and scallions to squash and mix well. Create "tot" shapes with your hands and place in air fryer. Spray with olive oil. Cook 15 minutes at 350 degrees until golden and crispy!

Nutrition: Calories: 231 Fat: 18g Protein: 5g Sugar: 0g

216. CINNAMON BUTTERNUT SQUASH FRIES

PREPARATION TIME
10 MINUTES

COOK TIME
10

SERVING
2

INGREDIENTS

- 1 pinch of salt
- 1 tbsp. powdered unprocessed sugar
- 2 tsp. cinnamon
- 1 tbsp. coconut oil
- 10 ounces pre-cut butternut squash fries

DIRECTIONS

1. In a plastic bag, pour in all ingredients. Coat fries with other components till coated and sugar is dissolved. Spread coated fries into a single layer in the air fryer. Cook 10 minutes at 390 degrees until crispy.

Nutrition: Calories: 175 Fat: 8g Protein: 1g Sugar: 5g

217. CHEESY ROASTED SWEET POTATOES

PREPARATION TIME 5 MINUTES
COOK TIME 20
SERVING 4

INGREDIENTS

- 2 large sweet potatoes, peeled and sliced
- 1 teaspoon olive oil
- 1 tablespoon white balsamic vinegar
- 1 teaspoon dried thyme
- ¼ cup grated Parmesan cheese

DIRECTIONS

1. In a big bowl, shower the sweet potato slices with the olive oil and toss.
2. Sprinkle with the balsamic vinegar and thyme and toss again.
3. Sprinkle the potatoes with the Parmesan cheese and toss to coat.
4. Roast the slices, in batches, in the air fryer basket for 18 to 23 minutes, tossing the sweet potato slices in the basket once during cooking, until tender.
5. Repeat with the remaining sweet potato slices. Serve immediately.

Nutrition: Calories: 100; Fat: 3g Protein: 4g; Carbohydrates: 15g; Sodium: 132mg

218. SALTY LEMON ARTICHOKES

PREPARATION TIME
15 MINUTES

COOK TIME
45

SERVING
2

INGREDIENTS

- 1 lemon
- 2 artichokes
- 1 teaspoon kosher salt
- 1 garlic head
- 2 teaspoon olive oil

DIRECTIONS

1. Cut off the edges of the artichokes.
2. Cut the lemon into the halves.
3. Peel the garlic head and chop the garlic cloves roughly.
4. Then place the chopped garlic in the artichokes.
5. Sprinkle the artichokes with the olive oil and kosher salt.
6. Then squeeze the lemon juice into the artichokes.
7. Wrap the artichokes in the foil.
8. Preheat the air fryer to 330 F.
9. Place the wrapped artichokes in the air fryer and cook for 45 minutes.
10. When the artichokes are cooked; discard the foil and serve.
11. Enjoy!

Nutrition: Calories 133, Fat 5, Fiber 9.7, Carbs 21.7, Protein 6

219. ASPARAGUS & PARMESAN

PREPARATION TIME
10 MINUTES

COOK TIME
6

SERVING
2

INGREDIENTS

- 1 teaspoon sesame oil
- 11 oz asparagus
- 1 teaspoon chicken stock
- ½ teaspoon ground white pepper
- 3 oz Parmesan

DIRECTIONS

1. Wash the asparagus and chop it roughly.
2. Sprinkle the chopped asparagus with the chicken stock and ground white pepper.
3. Then sprinkle the vegetables with the sesame oil and shake them.
4. Place the asparagus in the air fryer basket.
5. Cook the vegetables for 4 minutes at 400 F.
6. Meanwhile, shred Parmesan cheese.
7. When the time is over; shake the asparag
8. p
9. us gently and sprinkle with the shredded cheese.
10. Cook the asparagus for 2 minutes more at 400 F.
11. After this, transfer the cooked asparagus in the serving plates.
12. Serve and taste it!

Nutrition: Calories 189, Fat 11.6, Fiber 3.4, Carbs 7.9 Protein 17.2

220. CORN ON COBS

PREPARATION TIME
10 MINUTES

COOK TIME
10

SERVING
2

INGREDIENTS

- 2 fresh corn on cobs
- 2 teaspoon butter
- 1 teaspoon salt
- 1 teaspoon paprika
- ¼ teaspoon olive oil

DIRECTIONS

1. Preheat the air fryer to 400 F.
2. Rub the corn on cobs with the salt and paprika.
3. Then sprinkle the corn on cobs with the olive oil.
4. Place the corn on cobs in the air fryer basket.
5. Cook the corn on cobs for 10 minutes.
6. When the time is over; transfer the corn on cobs in the serving plates and rub with the butter gently.
7. Serve the meal immediately.
8. Enjoy!

Nutrition: Calories: 289 kcal/Cal, Carbs: 12.8 g, Fat: 32 g, Protein: 21.1 g

221. ONION GREEN BEANS

PREPARATION TIME
10 MINUTES

COOK TIME
12

SERVING
2

INGREDIENTS

- 11 oz green beans
- 1 tablespoon onion powder
- 1 tablespoon olive oil
- ½ teaspoon salt
- ¼ teaspoon chili flakes

DIRECTIONS

1. Wash the green beans carefully and place them in the bowl.
2. Sprinkle the green beans with the onion powder, salt, chili flakes, and olive oil.
3. Shake the green beans carefully.
4. Preheat the air fryer to 400 F.
5. Put the green beans in the air fryer and cook for 8 minutes.
6. After this, shake the green beans and cook them for 4 minutes more at 400 F.
7. When the time is over; shake the green beans.
8. Serve the side dish and enjoy!

Nutrition: Calories 1205, Fat 7.2, Fiber 5.5, Carbs 13.9, Protein 3.2

222. DILL MASHED POTATO

PREPARATION TIME
10 MINUTES

COOK TIME
12

SERVING
2

INGREDIENTS

- 2 potatoes
- 2 tablespoon fresh dill, chopped
- 1 teaspoon butter
- ½ teaspoon salt
- ¼ cup half and half

DIRECTIONS

1. Preheat the air fryer to 390 F.
2. Rinse the potatoes thoroughly and place them in the air fryer.
3. Cook the potatoes for 15 minutes.
4. After this, remove the potatoes from the air fryer.
5. Peel the potatoes.
6. Mash the potatoes with the help of the fork well.
7. Then add chopped fresh dill and salt.
8. Stir it gently and add butter and half and half.
9. Take the hand blender and blend the mixture well.
10. When the mashed potato is cooked; serve it immediately. Enjoy!

Nutrition: Calories 211, Fat 5.7, Fiber 5.5, Carbs 36.5, Protein 5.1

223. CREAM POTATO

PREPARATION TIME
15 MINUTES

COOK TIME
20

SERVING
2

INGREDIENTS

- 3 medium potatoes, scrubbed
- ½ teaspoon kosher salt
- 1 tablespoon Italian seasoning
- 1/3 cup cream
- ½ teaspoon ground black pepper

DIRECTIONS

1. Slice the potatoes.
2. Preheat the air fryer to 365 F.
3. Make the layer from the sliced potato in the air fryer basket.
4. Sprinkle the potato layer with the kosher salt and ground black pepper.
5. After this, make the second layer of the potato and sprinkle it with Italian seasoning.
6. Make the last layer of the sliced potato and pour the cream.
7. Cook the scallop potato for 20 minutes.
8. When the scalloped potato is cooked; let it chill till the room temperature. Enjoy!

Nutrition: Calories 269, Fat 4.7, Fiber 7.8, Carbs 52.6, Protein 5.8

224. CHARD WITH CHEDDAR

PREPARATION TIME
10 MINUTES

COOK TIME
11

SERVING
2

INGREDIENTS

- 3 oz Cheddar cheese, grated
- 10 oz Swiss chard
- 3 tablespoon cream
- 1 tablespoon sesame oil
- salt and pepper to taste

DIRECTIONS

1. Wash Swiss chard carefully and chop it roughly.
2. After this, sprinkle chopped Swiss chard with the salt and ground white pepper.
3. Stir it carefully.
4. Sprinkle Swiss chard with the sesame oil and stir it carefully with the help of 2 spatulas.
5. Preheat the air fryer to 260 F.
6. Put chopped Swiss chard in the air fryer basket and cook for 6 minutes.
7. Shake it after 3 minutes of cooking.
8. Then pour the cream into the air fryer basket and mix it up.
9. Cook the meal for 3 minutes more.
10. Then increase the temperature to 400 F.
11. Sprinkle the meal with the grated cheese and cook for 2 minutes more.
12. After this, transfer the meal in the serving plates. Enjoy!

Nutrition: Calories 272, Fat 22.3, Fiber 2.5, Carbs 6.7, Protein 13.3

225. CHILI SQUASH WEDGES

PREPARATION TIME
10 MINUTES

COOK TIME
18

SERVING
2

INGREDIENTS

- 11 oz Acorn squash
- ½ teaspoon salt
- tablespoon olive oil
- ½ teaspoon chili pepper
- ½ teaspoon paprika

DIRECTIONS

1. Cut Acorn squash into the serving wedges.
2. Sprinkle the wedges with the salt, olive oil, chili pepper, and paprika.
3. Massage the wedges gently.
4. Preheat the air fryer to 400 F.
5. Put Acorn squash wedges in the air fryer basket and cook for 18 minutes.
6. Flip the wedges into another side after 9 minutes of cooking.
7. Serve the cooked meal hot. Enjoy!

Nutrition: Calories 125, Fat 7.2, Fiber 2.6, Carbs 16.7, Protein 1.4

226. HONEY CARROTS WITH GREENS

PREPARATION TIME
7 MINUTES

COOK TIME
12

SERVING
2

INGREDIENTS

- 1 cup baby carrot
- ½ teaspoon salt
- ½ teaspoon white pepper
- 1 tablespoon honey
- 1 teaspoon sesame oil

DIRECTIONS

1. Preheat the air fryer to 385 F.
2. Combine the baby carrot with the salt, white pepper, and sesame oil.
3. Shake the baby carrot and transfer in the air fryer basket.
4. Cook the vegetables for 10 minutes.
5. After this, add honey and shake the vegetables.
6. Cook the meal for 2 minutes.
7. After this, shake the vegetables and serve immediately.
8. Enjoy!

Nutrition: Calories 83, Fat 2.4, Fiber 2.6, Carbs 16, Protein 0.6

227. SOUTH ASIAN CAULIFLOWER FRITTERS

PREPARATION TIME 5 MINUTES

COOK TIME 20

SERVING 4

INGREDIENTS

- 1 large chopped into florets cauliflower
- 3 tablespoons of Greek yogurt
- 3 tablespoons of flour
- ½ teaspoon of ground turmeric
- ½ teaspoon of ground cumin
- ½ teaspoon of ground paprika
- 12 teaspoon of ground coriander
- ½ teaspoon of salt
- ½ teaspoon of black pepper

DIRECTIONS

1. Using a large bowl, add and mix the Greek yogurt, flour, and seasonings properly.
2. Add the cauliflower florets and toss it until it is well covered
3. Heat up your air fryer to 390 degrees Fahrenheit.
4. Grease your air fryer basket with a nonstick cooking spray and add half of the cauliflower florets to it.
5. Cook it for 10 minutes or until it turns golden brown and crispy, then shake it after 5 minutes. (Repeat this with the other half).
6. Serve and enjoy!

Nutrition: Calories: 120, Fat: 4g, Protein: 7.5g, Carbohydrates: 14g, Dietary Fiber: 3.4g

228. SUPREME AIR-FRIED TOFU

PREPARATION TIME
5 MINUTES

COOK TIME
50

SERVING
4

INGREDIENTS

- 1 block of pressed and sliced into 1-inch cubes of extra-firm tofu
- 2 tablespoons of soy sauce
- 1 teaspoon of seasoned rice vinegar
- 2 teaspoons of toasted sesame oil
- 1 tablespoon of cornstarch

DIRECTIONS

1. Using a bowl, add and toss the tofu, soy sauce, seasoned rice vinegar, sesame oil until it is properly covered.
2. Place it inside your refrigerator and allow to marinate for 30 minutes.
3. Preheat your air fryer to 370 degrees Fahrenheit.
4. Add the cornstarch to the tofu mixture and toss it until it is properly covered.
5. Grease your air fryer basket with a nonstick cooking spray and add the tofu inside your basket.
6. Cook it for 20 minutes at a 370 degrees Fahrenheit, and shake it after 10 minutes.
7. Serve and enjoy!

Nutrition: Calories: 80, Fat: 5.8g, Protein: 5g, Carbohydrates: 3g, Dietary Fiber: 1.2g

229. CRISPY POTATOES AND PARSLEY

PREPARATION TIME 10 MINUTES
COOK TIME 10
SERVING 4

INGREDIENTS

- 1-pound gold potatoes, cut into wedges
- Salt and black pepper to the taste
- 2 tablespoons olive
- Juice from ½ lemon
- ¼ cup parsley leaves, chopped

DIRECTIONS

1. Rub potatoes with salt, pepper, lemon juice and olive oil, put them in your air fryer and cook at 350 degrees F for 10 minutes. Divide among plates, sprinkle parsley on top and serve. Enjoy!

Nutrition: Calories 152, Fat 3, Fiber 7, Carbs 17, Protein 4

230. GARLIC TOMATOES

PREPARATION TIME
10 MINUTES

COOK TIME
15

SERVING
4

INGREDIENTS

- 4garlic cloves, crushed
- 1-pound mixed cherry tomatoes
- 3thyme springs, chopped
- Salt and black pepper to the taste
- ¼ cup olive oil

DIRECTIONS

1. In a bowl, mix tomatoes with salt, black pepper, garlic, olive oil and thyme, toss to coat, introduce in your air fryer and cook at 360 degrees F for 15 minutes. Divide tomatoes mix on plates and serve. Enjoy!

Nutrition: Calories 100, Fat 0, Fiber 1, Carbs 1, Protein 6

231. EASY GREEN BEANS AND POTATOES

PREPARATION TIME
10 MINUTES

COOK TIME
15

SERVING
5

INGREDIENTS

- 2pounds green beans
- 6new potatoes, halved
- Salt and black pepper to the taste
- A drizzle of olive oil
- 6bacon slices, cooked and chopped

DIRECTIONS

1. In a bowl, mix green beans with potatoes, salt, pepper and oil, toss, transfer to your air fryer and cook at 390 degrees F for 15 minutes. Divide among plates and serve with bacon sprinkled on top. Enjoy!

Nutrition: Calories 374, Fat 15, Fiber 12, Carbs 28, Protein 12

232. GREEN BEANS AND TOMATOES

PREPARATION TIME
10 MINUTES

COOK TIME
15

SERVING
4

INGREDIENTS

- 1 pint cherry tomatoes
- 1 pound green beans
- 2 tablespoons olive oil
- Salt and black pepper to the taste

DIRECTIONS

1. In a bowl, mix cherry tomatoes with green beans, olive oil, salt and pepper, toss, transfer to your air fryer and cook at 400 degrees F for 15 minutes. Divide among plates and serve right away. Enjoy!

Nutrition: Calories 162, Fat 6, Fiber 5, Carbs 8, Protein 9

9. DESSERTS

233. DONUTS PUDDING

PREPARATION TIME
15 MINUTES

COOK TIME
1 H

SERVING
6

INGREDIENTS

- glazed donuts, cut into small pieces
- ¾ cup frozen sweet cherries
- ½ cup raisins
- ½ cup semi-sweet chocolate baking chips.
- ¼ cup sugar
- 1 teaspoon ground cinnamon
- egg yolks
- 1½ cups whipping cream

DIRECTIONS

1. In a large bowl, mix together the donut pieces, cherries, raisins, chocolate chips, sugar, and cinnamon.
2. In another bowl, add the egg yolks, and whipping cream and whisk until well combined.
3. Add the egg yolk mixture into doughnut mixture and mix well.
4. Line a baking dish with a piece of foil.
5. Place donuts mixture into the prepared baking pan.
6. Press "power button" of air fry oven and turn the dial to select the "air fry" mode.
7. Press the time button and again turn the dial to set the Cooking Time: to 60 minutes.
8. Now push the temp button and rotate the dial to set the temperature at 360 degrees f.
9. Press "start/pause" button to start.
10. When the unit beeps to show that it is preheated, open the lid.
11. Arrange the pan in "air fry basket" and insert in the oven.
12. Place the pan onto a wire rack to cool for about 10-15 minutes before serving.
13. Serve warm.

Nutrition: Calories 537 Total fat 28.7 g Saturated fat 12.2 g Cholesterol 173 mg Sodium 194 mg Total carbs 65.1 g Fiber 2.3 g Sugar 32.8 g Protein 6.5 g

234. LEMON BARS

PREPARATION TIME
10 MINUTES

COOK TIME
35

SERVING
8

INGREDIENTS

- ½ cup butter, melted
- 1 cup erythritol
- 1 and ¾ cups almond flour
- 3eggs, whisked
- Juice of 3 lemons

DIRECTIONS

1. In a bowl, mix 1 cup flour with half of the erythritol and the butter, stir well and press into a baking dish that fits the air fryer lined with parchment paper.
2. Put the dish in your air fryer and cook at 350 degrees F for 10 minutes.
3. For the meantime, in a bowl, blend the rest of the flour with the remaining erythritol and the other ingredients and whisk well.
4. Spread this over the crust, put the dish in the air fryer once more and cook at 350 degrees F for 25 minutes.
5. Cool down, cut into bars and serve.

Nutrition: Calories; 210 Protein; 8 g. Fat; 12 g. Carbs; 4 g.

235. COCONUT DONUTS

PREPARATION TIME
5 MINUTES

COOK TIME
15

SERVING
4

INGREDIENTS

- 8ounces coconut flour
- 1 egg, whisked
- and ½ tablespoons butter, melted
- 4ounces coconut milk
- 1 teaspoon baking powder

DIRECTIONS

1. In a bowl, put all of the ingredients and mix well.
2. Shape donuts from this mix, place them in your air fryer's basket and cook at 370 degrees F for 15 minutes.
3. Serve warm.

Nutrition: Calories; 190 Protein; 6 g. Fat; 12 g. Carbs; 4 g.

236. BLUEBERRY CREAM

PREPARATION TIME
4 MINUTES

COOK TIME
20

SERVING
6

INGREDIENTS

- 2cups blueberries
- Juice of ½ lemon
- 2tablespoons water
- 1 teaspoon vanilla extract
- 2tablespoons swerve

DIRECTIONS

1. In a large bowl, put all ingredients and mix well.
2. Divide this into 6 ramekins, put them in the air fryer and cook at 340 degrees F for 20 minutes
3. Cool down and serve.

Nutrition: Calories; 123 Protein; 3 g. Fat; 2 g. Carbs; 4 g.

237. BLACKBERRY CHIA JAM

PREPARATION TIME
10 MINUTES

COOK TIME
30

SERVING
12

INGREDIENTS

- 3 cups blackberries
- ¼ cup swerve
- 4 tablespoons lemon juice
- 4 tablespoons chia seeds

DIRECTIONS

1. In a pan that suits the air fryer, combine all the Ingredients: and toss.
2. Put the pan in the fryer and cook at 300 degrees F for 30 minutes.
3. Divide into cups and serve cold.

Nutrition: Calories; 100 Protein; 1 g. Fat; 2 g. Carbs; 3 g.

238. MIXED BERRIES CREAM

PREPARATION TIME
5 MINUTES

COOK TIME
30

SERVING
6

INGREDIENTS

- 12ounces blackberries
- 6ounces raspberries
- 12ounces blueberries
- ¾ cup swerve
- 2ounces coconut cream

DIRECTIONS

1. In a bowl, put all the Ingredients: and mix well.
2. Divide this into 6 ramekins, put them in your air fryer and cook at 320 degrees F for 30 minutes.
3. Cool down and serve it.

Nutrition: Calories; 100 Protein; 2 g. Fat; 1 g. Carbs; 2 g.

239. BLOOD ORANGE AND GINGER CHEESECAKE

PREPARATION TIME 10 MINUTES

COOK TIME 45

SERVING 10

INGREDIENTS

- 1 cup almond flour
- 1/2 stick butter, melted
- 7 ounces Neufchatel, at room temperature
- 1/4 cup sour cream
- 8 ounces erythritol, powdered
- 2 eggs
- 2 tablespoons orange juice
- 1 teaspoon orange peel, finely shredded
- A pinch of salt
- A pinch of freshly grated nutmeg
- 1 teaspoon ground star anise
- 1/2 teaspoon vanilla paste
- 2 large blood oranges
- 2 tablespoons crystallized ginger, finely chopped

DIRECTIONS

1. Start by preheating your Air Fryer to 350 degrees F for 5 minutes. Coat the inside of a springform pan with a baking paper.
2. Then, in a mixing dish, thoroughly combine the almond flour with the butter. Press this crust into the bottom of a springform pan.
3. In a mixing dish, thoroughly combine the Neufchatel with the sour cream and erythritol. Fold in the eggs, one at a time and continue to whisk this mixture.
4. Add the orange juice and peel; add all seasonings. Spread this orange layer over the crust in the pan.
5. Place the springform pan into your Air Fryer; cook for 13 minutes; then, cook for a further 13 minutes at 320 degrees F,
6. Lastly, turn the temperature to 305 degrees F and cook an additional 17 minutes. Garnish with the blood orange and crystallized ginger.
7. Refrigerate overnight and serve well-chilled.

Nutrition: Calories; 201 Fat; 16.4g Carbs 7.1g Protein; 6.3g

240. SPICED PEAR SAUCE

PREPARATION TIME
10 MINUTES

COOK TIME
6 H

SERVING
12

INGREDIENTS

- 8 pears, cored and diced
- 1/2 tsp ground cinnamon
- 1/4 tsp ground nutmeg
- 1/4 tsp ground cardamom
- 1 cup of water

DIRECTIONS

1. Put all of the ingredients in the air fryer and stir well.
2. Seal the pot with a lid and select slow cook mode and cook on low for 6 hours.
3. Mash the sauce using potato masher.
4. Pour into the container and store.

Nutrition: Calories; 81 Protein; 0.5 g. Fat; 0.2 g. Carbs; 21.4 g.

241. HONEY FRUIT COMPOTE

PREPARATION TIME
10 MINUTES

COOK TIME
3

SERVING
4

INGREDIENTS

- 1/3 cup honey
- 1 1/2 cups blueberries
- 1 1/2 cups raspberries

DIRECTIONS

1. Put all of the ingredients in the air fryer basket and stir well.
2. Seal pot with lid and cook on high for 3 minutes.
3. Once done, allow to release pressure naturally. Remove lid.
4. Serve and enjoy.

Nutrition: Calories; 141 Protein; 1 g Fat; 0.5 g. Carbs; 36.7 g.

242. APRICOT CRUMBLE WITH BLACKBERRIES

PREPARATION TIME
30 MINUTES

COOK TIME
14

SERVING
4

INGREDIENTS

- ½ cups fresh apricots, de-stoned and cubed
- 1 cup fresh blackberries
- ½ cup sugar
- tbsp lemon juice
- 1 cup flour
- Salt as needed
- tbsp butter

DIRECTIONS

1. Add the apricot cubes to a bowl and mix with lemon juice, 2 tbsp sugar, and blackberries. Scoop the mixture into a greased dish and spread it evenly. In another bowl, mix flour and remaining sugar.
2. Add 1 tbsp of cold water and butter and keep mixing until you have a crumbly mixture. Preheat breville on bake function to 390 f and place the fruit mixture in the basket. Top with crumb mixture and cook for 20 minutes.

Nutrition: Calories: 546, Protein: 7g, Fat: 5.23g, Carbs: 102.53g

243. APPLE & CINNAMON PIE

PREPARATION TIME
30 MINUTES

COOK TIME
14

SERVING
9

INGREDIENTS

- apples, diced
- oz. butter, melted
- oz. sugar
- 1 oz. brown sugar
- tsp cinnamon
- 1 egg, beaten
- large puff pastry sheets
- ¼ tsp salt

DIRECTIONS

1. Whisk white sugar, brown sugar, cinnamon, salt, and butter, together. Place the apples in a baking dish and coat them with the mixture. Place the baking dish in the toaster oven, and cook for 10 minutes at 350 f on bake function.
2. Meanwhile, roll out the pastry on a floured flat surface, and cut each sheet into 6 equal pieces. Divide the apple filling between the pieces. Brush the edges of the pastry squares with the egg.
3. Fold them and seal the edges with a fork. Place on a lined baking sheet and cook in the fryer at 350 f for 8 minutes. Flip over, increase the temperature to 390 f, and cook for 2 more minutes.

Nutrition: Calories: 140, Protein: 1.28g, Fat: 6.33g, Carbs: 21.19g

244. MINI CHEESECAKES

PREPARATION TIME
15 MINUTES

COOK TIME
10

SERVING
2

INGREDIENTS

- ¾ cup erythritol
- eggs
- 1 teaspoon vanilla extract
- ½ teaspoon fresh lemon juice
- oz. Cream cheese, softened
- tablespoon sour cream

DIRECTIONS

1. In a blender, add the erythritol, eggs, vanilla extract and lemon juice and pulse until smooth.
2. Add the cream cheese and sour cream and pulse until smooth.
3. Place the mixture into 2 (4-inch) spring form pans evenly.
4. Press "power button" of air fry oven and turn the dial to select the "air fry" mode.
5. Press the time button and again turn the dial to set the Cooking Time: to 10 minutes.
6. Now push the temp button and rotate the dial to set the temperature at 350 degrees f.
7. Press "start/pause" button to start.
8. When the unit beeps to show that it is preheated, open the lid.
9. Arrange the pans in "air fry basket" and insert in the oven.
10. Place the pans onto a wire rack to cool completely.
11. Refrigerate overnight before serving.

Nutrition: Calories 886 Total fat 86 g Saturated fat 52.8 g Cholesterol 418 mg Sodium 740 mg Total carbs 7.2g Fiber 0 g Sugar 1.1 g Protein 23.1 g

245. VANILLA CHEESECAKE

PREPARATION TIME
15 MINUTES

COOK TIME
14

SERVING
6

INGREDIENTS

- 1 cup honey graham cracker crumbs
- tablespoons unsalted butter, softened
- 1 (453.592g). Cream cheese, softened
- ½ cup sugar
- large eggs
- ½ teaspoon vanilla extract

DIRECTIONS

1. Line a round baking pan with parchment paper.
2. For crust: in a bowl, add the graham cracker crumbs, and butter.
3. Place the crust into baking dish and press to smooth.
4. Press "power button" of air fry oven and turn the dial to select the "air fry" mode.
5. Press the time button and again turn the dial to set the Cooking Time: to 4 minutes.
6. Now push the temp button and rotate the dial to set the temperature at 350 degrees f.
7. Press "start/pause" button to start.
8. When the unit beeps to show that it is preheated, open the lid.
9. Arrange the baking pan of crust in "air fry basket" and insert in the oven.
10. Place the crust aside to cool for about 10 minutes.
11. Meanwhile, in a bowl, add the cream cheese, and sugar and whisk until smooth.
12. Now, place the eggs, one at a time and whisk until mixture becomes creamy.
13. Add the vanilla extract and mix well.
14. Place the cream cheese mixture evenly over the crust.
15. Press "power button" of air fry oven and turn the dial to select the "air fry" mode.
16. Press the time button and again turn the dial to set the Cooking Time: to 10 minutes.
17. Now push the temp button and rotate the dial to set the temperature at 350 degrees f.
18. Press "start/pause" button to start.
19. When the unit beeps to show that it is preheated, open the lid.
20. Arrange the baking pan of crust in "air fry basket" and insert in the oven.
21. Place the pan onto a wire rack to cool completely.
22. Refrigerate overnight before serving.

Nutrition: Calories 470 Total fat 33.9 g Saturated fat 20.6 g Cholesterol 155 mg Sodium 42 mg Total carbs 34.9 g Fiber 0.5 g Sugar 22 g Protein 9.4 g

246. RICOTTA CHEESECAKE

PREPARATION TIME
15 MINUTES

COOK TIME
25

SERVING
8

INGREDIENTS

- 17.6 oz. Ricotta cheese
- eggs
- ¾ cup sugar
- tablespoons corn starch
- 1 tablespoon fresh lemon juice
- teaspoons vanilla extract
- 1 teaspoon fresh lemon zest, finely grated

DIRECTIONS

1. In a large bowl, place all ingredients and mix until well combined.
2. Place the mixture into a baking pan.
3. Press "power button" of air fry oven and turn the dial to select the "air fry" mode.
4. Press the time button and again turn the dial to set the Cooking Time: to 25 minutes.
5. Now push the temp button and rotate the dial to set the temperature at 320 degrees f.
6. Press "start/pause" button to start.
7. When the unit beeps to show that it is preheated, open the lid.
8. Arrange the pan in "air fry basket" and insert in the oven.
9. Place the cake pan onto a wire rack to cool completely.
10. Refrigerate overnight before serving.

Nutrition: Calories 197 Total fat 6.6 g Saturated fat 3.6 g Cholesterol 81 mg Sodium 102 mg Total carbs 25.7g Fiber 0 g Sugar 19.3 g Protein 9.2 g

247. PECAN PIE

PREPARATION TIME
15 MINUTES

COOK TIME
35

SERVING
5

INGREDIENTS

- ¾ cup brown sugar
- ¼ cup caster sugar
- 1/3 cup butter, melted
- large eggs
- 1¾ tablespoons flour
- 1 tablespoon milk
- 1 teaspoon vanilla extract
- 1 cup pecan halves
- 1 frozen pie crust, thawed

DIRECTIONS

1. In a large bowl, mix together the sugars, and butter.
2. Add the eggs and whisk until foamy.
3. Add the flour, milk, and vanilla extract and whisk until well combined.
4. Fold in the pecan halves.
5. Grease a pie pan.
6. Arrange the crust in the bottom of prepared pie pan.
7. Place the pecan mixture over the crust evenly.
8. Press "power button" of air fry oven and turn the dial to select the "air fry" mode.
9. Press the time button and again turn the dial to set the Cooking Time: to 22 minutes.
10. Now push the temp button and rotate the dial to set the temperature at 300 degrees f.
11. Press "start/pause" button to start.
12. When the unit beeps to show that it is preheated, open the lid.
13. Arrange the pan in "air fry basket" and insert in the oven.
14. After 22 minutes of cooking, to set the temperature at w85 degrees f for 13 minutes.
15. Place the pie pan onto a wire rack to cool for about 10-15 minutes before serving.

Nutrition: Calories 501 Total fat 35 g Saturated fat 10.8 g Cholesterol 107 mg Sodium 187 mg Total carbs 44.7 g Fiber 2.9 g Sugar 36.7 g Protein 6.2 g

248. FRUITY CRUMBLE

PREPARATION TIME
15 MINUTES

COOK TIME
20

SERVING
4

INGREDIENTS

- ½ lb. (226.8g) Fresh apricots, pitted and cubed
- 1 cup fresh blackberries
- 1/3 cup sugar, divided
- 1 tablespoon fresh lemon juice
- 7/8 cup flour
- Pinch of salt
- 1 tablespoon cold water
- ¼ cup chilled butter, cubed

DIRECTIONS

1. Grease a baking pan.
2. In a large bowl, mix well apricots, blackberries, 2 tablespoons of sugar, and lemon juice.
3. Spread apricot mixture into the prepared baking pan.
4. In another bowl, add the flour, remaining sugar, salt, water, and butter and mix until a crumbly mixture form.
5. Spread the flour mixture over apricot mixture evenly.
6. Press "power button" of air fry oven and turn the dial to select the "air fry" mode.
7. Press the time button and again turn the dial to set the Cooking Time: to 20 minutes.
8. Now push the temp button and rotate the dial to set the temperature at 390 degrees f.
9. Press "start/pause" button to start.
10. When the unit beeps to show that it is preheated, open the lid.
11. Arrange the pan in "air fry basket" and insert in the oven.
12. Place the pan onto a wire rack to cool for about 10-15 minutes before serving.

Nutrition: Calories 307 Total fat 12.4 g Saturated fat 7.4 g Cholesterol 31 mg Sodium 123 mg Total carbs 47.3 g Fiber 3.8 g Sugar 23.7 g Protein 4.2 g

249. CHERRY CLAFOUTIS

PREPARATION TIME
15 MINUTES

COOK TIME
25

SERVING
4

INGREDIENTS

- 1½ cups fresh cherries, pitted
- tablespoons vodka
- ¼ cup flour
- tablespoons sugar
- Pinch of salt
- ½ cup sour cream
- 1 egg
- 1 tablespoon butter
- ¼ cup powdered sugar

DIRECTIONS

1. In a bowl, mix together the cherries and vodka.
2. In another bowl, mix together the flour, sugar, and salt.
3. Add the sour cream, and egg and mix until a smooth dough form.
4. Grease a cake pan.
5. Place flour mixture evenly into the prepared cake pan.
6. Spread cherry mixture over the dough.
7. Place butter on top in the form of dots.
8. Press "power button" of air fry oven and turn the dial to select the "air fry" mode.
9. Press the time button and again turn the dial to set the Cooking Time: to 25 minutes.
10. Now push the temp button and rotate the dial to set the temperature at 355 degrees f.
11. Press "start/pause" button to start.
12. When the unit beeps to show that it is preheated, open the lid.
13. Arrange the pan in "air fry basket" and insert in the oven.
14. Place the pan onto a wire rack to cool for about 10-15 minutes before serving.
15. Now, invert the clafoutis onto a platter and sprinkle with powdered sugar.
16. Cut the clafoutis into desired size slices and serve warm.

Nutrition: Calories 241 Total fat 10.1 g Saturated fat 5.9 g Cholesterol 61 mg Sodium 90 mg Total carbs 29 g Fiber 1.3 g Sugar 20.6 g Protein 3.9 g

250. APPLE BREAD PUDDING

PREPARATION TIME
15 MINUTES

COOK TIME
44

SERVING
8

INGREDIENTS

For bread pudding:
- 10½ oz. Bread, cubed
- ½ cup apple, peeled, cored and chopped
- ½ cup raisins
- ¼ cup walnuts, chopped
- 1½ cups milk
- ¾ cup water
- tablespoons honey
- teaspoons ground cinnamon
- teaspoons cornstarch
- 1 teaspoon vanilla extract

For topping:
- 1 1/3 cups plain flour
- 3/5 cup brown sugar
- tablespoons butter

DIRECTIONS

1. In a large bowl, mix together the bread, apple, raisins, and walnuts.
2. In another bowl, add the remaining pudding ingredients and mix until well combined.
3. Add the milk mixture into bread mixture and mix until well combined.
4. Refrigerate for about 15 minutes, tossing occasionally.
5. For topping: in a bowl, mix together the flour and sugar.
6. With a pastry cutter, cut in the butter until a crumbly mixture form.
7. Place the mixture into 2 baking pans and spread the topping mixture on top of each.
8. Press "power button" of air fry oven and turn the dial to select the "air fry" mode.
9. Press the time button and again turn the dial to set the Cooking Time: to 22 minutes.
10. Now push the temp button and rotate the dial and set the temperature at 355 degrees f.
11. Press "start/pause" button to start.
12. When the unit beeps to show that it is preheated, open the lid.
13. Arrange 1 pan in "air fry basket" and insert in the oven.
14. Place the pan onto a wire rack to cool slightly before serving.
15. Repeat with the remaining pan.
16. Serve warm.

Nutrition: Calories 432 Total fat 14.8 g Saturated fat 7.4 g Cholesterol 30 mg Sodium 353mg Total carbs 69.1 g Fiber 2.8 g Sugar 32 g Protein 7.9 g

251. MASALA CASHEW

PREPARATION TIME
25 MINUTES

COOK TIME
50

SERVING
2

INGREDIENTS

- 2 oz. Greek yogurt
- 1 tbsp mango powder
- 8¾ oz. cashew nuts
- Salt and pepper to taste
- 1 tsp coriander powder
- ½ tsp masala powder
- ½ tsp black pepper powder

DIRECTIONS

1. Preheat your Fryer to 240 F.
2. In a bowl, mix all powders. Season with salt and pepper.
3. Add cashews and toss to coat well.
4. Place the cashews in your air fryer's basket and cook for 15 minutes. Serve with a garnish of basil.

Nutrition: Calories: 202; Fat: 6; Fiber: 3; Carbs: 17; Protein: 10

CONCLUSION

Hopefully, after going through this book and trying out a couple of recipes, you will get to understand the flexibility and utility of the Breville smart air fryers. It is undoubtedly a multipurpose kitchen appliance that is highly recommended to everybody as it presents one with a palatable atmosphere to enjoy fried foods that are not only delicious but healthy, cheaper, and more convenient. The use of this kitchen appliance ensures that the making of some of your favorite snacks and meals will be carried out in a stress-free manner without hassling around, which invariably legitimizes its worth and gives you value for your money.

This book will be your all-time guide to understand the basics of the Breville smart air fryer because, with all the recipes mentioned in the book, you are sure that it will be something that you and the rest of the people around the world will enjoy for the rest of your lives. You will be able to prepare delicious and flavorsome meals that will not only be easy to carry out but tasty and healthy as well.

However, you should never limit yourself to the recipes solely mentioned in this cookbook, go on and try new things! Explore new recipes! Experiment with different ingredients, seasonings, and different methods! Create some new recipes and keep your mind open. By so doing, you will be able to get the best out of your Breville smart air fryer oven.

We are so glad you took the leap to this healthier cooking format with us!

The air fryer truly is not a gadget that should stay on the shelf. Instead, take it out and give it a whirl when you are whipping up one of your tried-and-true recipes, or if you are starting to get your feet wet with the air frying method.

Regardless of appliances, recipes, or dietary concerns, we hope you have fun in your kitchen. Between food preparation, cooking time, and then the cleanup, a lot of time is spent in this one room, so it should be as fun as possible.

This is just the start. There are no limits to working with the Breville smart air fryer, and we will explore some more recipes as well. In addition to all the great options that we talked about before, you will find that there are tasty desserts that can those sweet teeth in no time, and some great sauces and dressing so you can always be in control over the foods you eat. There are just so many options to choose from that it won't take long before you find a whole bunch of recipes to use, and before you start to wonder why you didn't get the Breville smart air fryer so much sooner. There are so many things to admire about the air fryer, and it becomes an even better tool to use when you have the right recipes in place and can use them. And there are so many fantastic recipes that work well in the air fryer and can get dinner on the table in no time. We are pleased that you pursue this Breville smart Air Fryer oven cookbook. Happy, healthy eating!

1 cup = 227g   8 oz
½ cup = 113.5g   4 oz
¾ cup = 170.3g   6 oz
2/3 cup 151.3g 5.3 oz

1 cup plain flour
1 tsp. baking powder
1 tsp. bicarb.
¼ tsp salt
1 egg
1/3 cup sugar
1 tsp vanilla
2 tbspoon butter melted
1½ cup mix-in of choice

1) small bowl mix flour, baking powder + salt
2) mix separate bowl egg, sugar, milk (yog) vanilla + butter
3) slowly add in flour
4) fold in fruit

7 muffins

320°F fr
12 mins
rotate 1.5
higher

CPSIA information can be obtained
at www.ICGtesting.com
Printed in the USA
LVHW061609210121
676908LV00038B/865